Showdown:
The Looming Crisis Over Gun Control

by Lenden A. Eakin

Showdown: The Looming Crisis Over Gun Control
Published by Mascot Books
560 Herndon Parkway #120, Herndon, VA 20170
Visit us on the Web at guncontrolbook.com

PRBVG1214A

ISBN: 978-1-63177-005-0
Library of Congress Control Number: 2014917085

Disclaimer:
A small portion of the material herein has been previously published as an e-book under the title *Disarming America.*

www.mascotbooks.com

Dedication

I dedicate this book to my father, Trooper G. Ralph Eakin
(1919-2010), Badge # 150, Virginia State Police,
my first teacher about law and firearms

and

The Citizen Soldiers of the 116th Infantry,
Virginia Army National Guard,
always ready, just in case.

Acknowledgements

First, I thank my wife, Kimberly,
for putting up with over a year's worth of my near daily disappearance
to work on this book.

The same goes for my office staff, especially Elaine and Charlotte,
without whom I could not have written it at all,
and my law partner, Ray Ferris,
who allowed me to use our staff.

My photographer, Maria Levitov,
and editors Dana Bell, Kevin Kays, and Jim Hall,
all deserve praise for their help,
as do Ron Kaye and Connie Schmidt
for their expert assistance
with book production and final edit.

Finally, many thanks to Rod Mitchell, the publicist who first put me
on national television and encouraged me to write *Showdown*
from before I began until its completion.

Table of Contents

Introduction

In mid-December 2012, I traveled for several days to work on a case involving the contested will of a disabled veteran. His family argued that a disability finding for mental health reasons and appointment of a trustee to manage his affairs proved that he did not have the mental capacity to make a will.

The veteran's drafting attorney, doctor, witnesses to the will, and the notary all thought that he had demonstrated capacity at the time he signed a will leaving his estate to friends and neighbors. The law requires that the maker of a will know his family, know the nature and extent of his assets and understand the contents of the will at the moment of signing for the will to be valid. Most of the witnesses lived several hours away, where the veteran's hometown attorney prepared the will. He had moved to my area after signing his will.

I had spent three long days interviewing witnesses, defending depositions, and traveling. I did not see or hear any news during that time. When I returned home after midnight, having driven for six hours in the rain, I found my family sleeping soundly. I turned on the television news to unwind after the long drive. That's when I first saw that, on the day before, a 20-year-old maniac named Adam Lanza had killed a room full of first graders in Newtown, Connecticut. This horrible news brought tears to my eyes. After drying them, I walked upstairs to hug my children, then ages six and eight, while they slept.

The next day, and for many weeks afterward, when I read or watched the news, much of the discussion involved the call for renewing the federal assault weapons ban. This made no sense to me, because the rifle involved already complied with Connecticut's long-standing assault weapons ban. Public figures focused even more on "universal" background checks in response to the shooting, but why? Lanza had killed his mother and stolen her guns, which were all legally sold to her after she had passed full background checks.

Why the lack of logic? I should have been hearing cries for secure storage of firearms, real solutions for protection from those with dangerous mental illnesses, and ideas for protecting our children at school. I could not understand the obsession with background checks and bans. They had already been in place for the Sandy Hook shooting, and making them a national requirement would have done absolutely nothing to prevent the Newtown tragedy.

I have followed the national and state debates about guns closely for two reasons. First, I hoped to see ideas that would actually make my children safer. Second, I have lived in the firearms community, or "gun culture," for decades, and I found the illogic that was so prevalent in the discussion both fascinating and appalling.

My father, a state police firearms instructor and national champion competitive shooter, began teaching me about guns as soon as I could walk. By my early teens, I knew how to cast bullets with a lead furnace and hand-held molds, as well as how to reload ammunition of all types. I had my own rifles (a .22 and a .243) and a shotgun (20 gauge), and practiced frequently. I had fired thousands of rounds with many different rifles and shotguns by the time I reached the age of 18, at which time I left for college and began Army R.O.T.C. training. During my time in the military, I repeatedly qualified as "Expert" with the M-16, and I often pulled Range Officer duty, as the officer in charge of rifle ranges.

After college, active duty Army service, and law school, I became a Federal Firearms Licensed dealer. This sideline included having regular exhibits at gun shows, where I made many of my sales. Later, I began teaching firearms safety and marksmanship with the Virginia's Hunter Education program and as an NRA instructor. I also handled a number of firearms-related legal matters, including litigation. During these years, I became very familiar with the history of the Second Amendment and related case law.

I understand the Second Amendment as a right that allows me, or any responsible citizen, to perform a historic duty. I have the *right* to "keep and bear" firearms, along with the accessories, ammunition, and other gear necessary to use them. I have a *duty* to learn how to use my firearms well and stand ready to act, at least temporarily, as a citizen soldier (militia) in defense of my family, community, and nation in case of need, such as in a crisis.

To me, the Second Amendment rights described by the President and many commentators seem to come from some other part of the world. What happened to the "common defense" purpose of the

Constitution? When did "weapons of war," or service rifles, become inappropriate for Americans to own? How did the extremely popular and commonly owned AR-15 fall into the "unusual" category? I had trouble understanding the rationale behind the public dialogue or "gun debate."

In recent years, due to my experience with law and firearms, I've been invited to be a guest speaker on radio talk shows all over the country, and have frequently accepted these invitations. The hosts often wanted my take on various legislative proposals or comments by prominent figures, and I occasionally answered questions called in by listeners, some of whom seemed frightened to the point of paranoia. My local NBC and CBS affiliates interviewed me on television. CNN placed me in a short debate with the spokesman for Mayors Against Illegal Guns on the Piers Morgan show. Local groups also asked me to speak about guns and the Second Amendment at their meetings and seminars.

I soon realized that the conflict between pressures for civilian disarmament and support of the Second Amendment had far more depth and complexity than anyone could address in the sound bites and short paragraphs of modern news. I began the research for this book as a result of that realization, in hopes that I could gain a more complete understanding of the conflict, and share that understanding with others. I wanted to learn both sides of the issues, analyzing each one as an attorney. Consequently, my writing mostly follows the style I would use to explain a case to a judge, with quotes, citations, and references for points of fact or law.

On one side of the debate, I found facts and efforts that surprised or even shocked me. The "anti-gun" effort had never drawn my full attention before. The "pro-gun" side held few if any surprises, but again, I have lived in that culture my entire life. The surprises I encountered on the anti-gun side included discovering a "playbook" or guide that advocates the use of tragedies to achieve anti-gun political goals. I also had no idea that our government faced such strong international pressures to disarm American citizens, especially from the European Union and the United Nations. Further, I did not realize that so many lawmakers, judges, and members of the Executive Branch, including the President, want to change or eliminate the Second Amendment and abandon its original purposes. I wondered what happened to their official oaths to "support and defend the Constitution."

I interviewed many non-gun owners and studied the comments of others to help me understand their perspective. I found that large numbers of intelligent, well-educated people have extremely unfavorable views of private firearms ownership. They often knew nothing about guns, except what they learned from movies, television shows, the news, and other media. Some had even stronger negative views because aside from what they had observed in the media, their sole experience came from working in hospital emergency rooms or criminal courtrooms, where the aftermath of the misuse of guns is on constant display. Many of these folks also believe that America should disarm all civilians, so that only the military and police have firearms.

The millions of people with negative views about guns probably did not have parents and other family who taught them about firearms. They most likely did not receive gun safety and marksmanship training from the Boy Scouts, 4-H, NRA-affiliated junior shooting clubs, or Hunter Education programs. Many truly do not understand why anyone other than law enforcement or military personnel would even want to own and shoot guns. They also believe that their families would be safer if America prohibited most gun ownership and reduced the firepower of any remaining civilian firearms.

I know from experience that most gun owners cannot fathom such negative views about guns. Sure, bad or crazy people can and do misuse them, but how does that differ from misuse of other dangerous objects? These "pro-gun" people do not comprehend why anyone would want to take away any of their guns. They include target shooters, hunters, collectors, and perhaps most importantly, those who want the ability to defend themselves and their families in the event of an attack.

Many millions of citizens with positive views on firearms live all of their adult lives with one or more guns close at hand. They often come from a long family tradition of having a weapon handy in case of emergency. Those with the strongest self-defense instincts live within arm's length of a gun nearly all of the time.

One of my relatives (a former Navy firearms instructor) put it like this: "My pistol is like a fire extinguisher. I keep it handy for sudden emergencies. My M-1A is more like a lifeboat. If things go really bad (like a sinking ship), I'll have it to help keep us (his family and community) safe."

These people often have a different gun tucked away within easy reach in their homes, cars, and offices. Some also have a concealed carry permit, and keep a pistol on their person. Regardless of how they maintain access to a weapon, millions of Americans become very upset at the thought of losing their means of defense and security.

The strong emotional element of the debate over firearms is what inspired me to call it a "gun control crisis." Sympathy for victims and fear of becoming a victim on one side clash with the desire for self-defense and acknowledgment of the importance of citizen soldiers on the other. Both sides expend almost unimaginable resources in the fight over guns.

This book will help gun owners and non-gun owners alike to better understand each other's point of view. The first chapter summarizes the history, law, and politics that bring us to the current legal situation regarding the Second Amendment. It tracks the high profile misuse of firearms that led to legislation, and describes the laws passed in response. The next chapter explains the reasons a great many Americans want to keep their arms, and to bear them when necessary. The third chapter discusses recent politics, including the failure of the Senate Gun Control Act of 2013, and proposals that are expected in the future.

The book goes on to briefly summarize the history of firearms and militia since the first permanent English settlement of Jamestown, Virginia in 1607, concluding with the current legal status of the militia. It also describes every prominent weapon used by militia in times of war. Then it explains the terms "assault rifle" and "assault weapon," with particular emphasis on the M-16 and AR-15. The book includes a hard look at bans of AR-15s and how they conflict with the Constitution, given the AR-15's status as the highly popular civilian version of America's current service rifle.

Another chapter describes each of the major issues in the "gun debate" and gives reasons for a lack of consensus or even the possibility of compromise. This chapter also addresses what appears to many to be an effort to completely disarm the American public and give government a monopoly over the power to resist violence with armed force.

The final chapter contains detailed, practical advice for anyone who needs information on how to exercise their Second Amendment rights. It also explains why we still have those rights today. I offer recommendations as to rifles, ammunition, accessories, clothing, gear, and other items one needs to function as a temporary soldier, as envisioned by the Second Amendment. I also suggest books, manuals, courses, classes, and activities for the training necessary to become an asset to the community in the event of a crisis that requires citizens to act for the common defense.

Ultimately, the American people will have to address and answer the question of whether we will continue to have arms to use as Citizen Soldiers in a crisis, or whether we will disarm civilians and become more like England and Australia, as President Obama suggests. It is my hope that what you read in this book will educate you, no matter where you stand politically. Then, when considering or discussing Second Amendment issues, you can speak as someone who understands the facts and the law on both sides of the argument.

Lenden A. Eakin

Chapter 1

A MODERN HISTORY OF VIOLENCE

The Reasons for Gun Control

This chapter surveys the violent acts that have given rise to gun control laws and references those laws. Our survey begins in 1934 with the Federal government's first attempt to limit citizens' rights to own firearms, and ends almost 80 years later with the Washington, D.C. Navy Yard shooting. In conclusion, it discusses the conflict between the American people's two very different reactions to violence. One reaction is the press for expanding gun control laws. The other reaction includes increased firearms sales, more concealed carry permit applications, and preparation for active defense by civilians.

National Firearms Act of 1934

Previous high profile violence by criminals with machine guns caused the 20th century's first gun control effort. The passage of this Act began the modern concept of "control" over guns by law. Its general acceptance by the public and the courts opened the door to more laws that try to reduce violence by restricting access to firearms.

World War I resulted in the development of two famous American made firearms, the misuse of which caused the first major federal gun control law. The fully automatic 1918 Browning Automatic Rifle (BAR) and 1921 Colt Thompson submachine gun, designed for assault against troops in trenches or to defend against mass attack, allowed the individual soldier to have substantially more fire power than a bolt action rifle. (The military eventually incorporated some of their features into every soldier's weapon by the end of the century.)

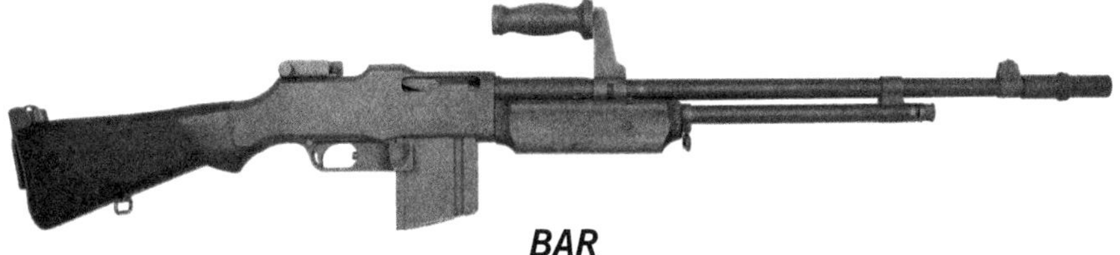

BAR

Gangster and other criminal use of the "Tommy Gun" and BAR caused great public fear of violence in the 1920s and early 1930s. Bonnie and Clyde, Al Capone and John Dillinger epitomized the problem. Criminals armed with Thompsons and BARs used them to rob banks, fight with police and murder rivals. FBI director J. Edgar Hoover helped orchestrate the passing of the National Firearms Act of 1934 in response.

This gun control measure required the registration of full automatic firearms, short barreled shotguns and short barreled rifles as well as payment of a $200.00 tax for each transfer of those guns. The tax exceeded the cost of a Thompson or a BAR at the time. While this law did not prevent wrongful use of these weapons, it made the possession alone a crime, unless registered with the Treasury Department.[1]

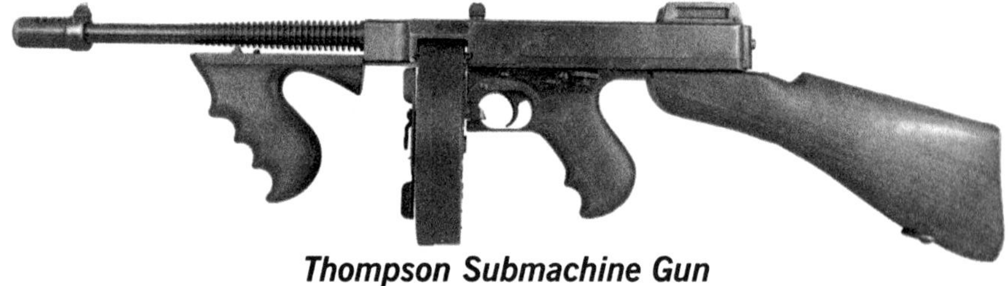

Thompson Submachine Gun

World War II saw the widespread use of the Thompson and the BAR by the military. This use was not considered "usual" in 1934, so the courts have deemed the National Firearms Act to be Constitutional, and not infringing on citizens' rights to ownership. Modern courts have concurred that full automatic rifles and submachine guns fall under the "dangerous and unusual weapons" category appropriate for restriction under the Second Amendment, in part because they have never been "commonly used" by civilians. Since civilians can only own certain registered models, courts have found them "unusual," as well as "dangerous."

The Supreme Court case of *U.S. v. Miller* used the "dangerous and unusual" concept to uphold convictions for possession of an unregistered sawed-off shotgun. The National Firearms Act applied to the short barreled shotgun. Noting that the shotgun in question did not fit the definition of weapons suitable for militia use, the Court upheld the "infringement" of the right to bear this particular arm.[2] Early English law included a prohibition against the carrying of dangerous and unusual weapons in public.[3] While the original intent of this law appeared to be a restriction on behavior ("carrying") rather than possession, the Miller Court used it to support the decision, which gave rise to the "common use" test for allowing restrictions on firearms ownership.[4]

Federal Firearms Act of 1938

A second law, the Federal Firearms Act of 1938 (F.F.A.), required dealers to have licenses to buy or sell firearms across state lines. It also mandated licenses for manufacturers and importers of firearms. This law prohibited sales to people under indictment for or convicted of violent felonies.[5]

John F. Kennedy

The first high profile act of violence that I recall happened a few days after my eighth birthday, on Friday, November 22, 1963. Lee Harvey Oswald used a surplus Italian military rifle to shoot President John F. Kennedy in the head as he rode in an open convertible at 12:30 p.m. that day. According to the Associated Press, "The President probably never heard the shot or knew what hit him."[6]

Our black and white television received two networks, NBC and CBS, where non-stop coverage of the shooting began immediately. Literally nothing else aired for days. From the assassination, to the funeral and shooting of the assassin, the print, radio and television media understandably made President Kennedy's death and its aftermath the world's biggest story.

Acting White House press secretary Malcolm Kilduff made the official announcement at 1:33 p.m. on Friday. He read a prepared statement: "President John F. Kennedy died at approximately 1 p.m. Central Standard Time today here in Dallas. He died of a gunshot wound in the brain."[7] My mother cried for days. My father did not say much, but I could tell that he also felt sad.

Ninety-eight minutes after Kennedy's death, Lyndon B. Johnson took the oath of office as President. Johnson's oath said: "I do solemnly swear that I will faithfully execute the office of the President of the United States, and will to the best of my ability preserve, protect and defend the Constitution of the United States. So help me God."[8]

Seven matching gray draft horses pulled a black-draped artillery caisson up White House Drive to wait for President Kennedy's body on Sunday, November 24. As the funeral procession formed at 12:20 p.m., newscasters announced that someone had shot Oswald outside the jail in Dallas.

The funeral cortege flowed down Pennsylvania Avenue from the White House to the Capitol, to the solemn beat of drums. The Joint Chiefs of Staff marched along. It included a black, riderless horse with polished cavalry boots reversed in the stirrups and a silver sword hanging from the empty saddle.

A black limousine carried the President's widow, Jacqueline, and young children, Caroline and John. Jackie Kennedy stepped out of the limo and walked most of the distance with her husband's casket. As the caisson reached the Capitol, the news announced the death of Lee Harvey Oswald. The same emergency medical staff who had tried to save the President in Dallas on Friday had also attended Oswald.

The 6.5x52mm Model 91-38 Italian Carcano bolt action rifle Oswald used had a telescopic sight and cost $19.95. He had purchased it through the mail using a false name.

Oswald had mental illness issues as a boy but never received treatment.[9]

After three years in the U.S. Marines, he pledged allegiance to the Soviet Union, where he lived for a while, then returned to the United States. While in Moscow he attempted suicide.[10] The Russians considered him "a crazy man who tried to kill himself."[11] We still do not know why he killed John F. Kennedy.

Oswald also killed Dallas police officer J.D. Tippit with a Smith and Wesson .38 Special revolver shortly after shooting Kennedy. Two days later, Jack Ruby assassinated Oswald outside Dallas Police headquarters with a nickel plated Colt Detective Special revolver, also in .38 Special caliber.

Texas Clock Tower

Charles Whitman stabbed his wife to death on the evening of July 31, 1966. Sometime later that night, he bludgeoned and stabbed his mother, killing her. The next morning he took a shotgun, three rifles, three pistols, and a footlocker full of supplies and other gear to the University of Texas. Whitman carried his weapons and equipment to the observation deck area of the University Clock Tower. On his way, he killed the receptionist by striking her twice in the head with a rifle butt.

Shortly after killing the receptionist, he shot several people with a shotgun as he climbed the steps to the Clock Tower observation deck, killing two and wounding two. Whitman proceeded to shoot 41 more people, killing 11 and wounding 30. Most of these shots were with a Remington Model 700 bolt action rifle in 6mm Remington caliber. He also had a Remington Model 141 pump action rifle in .35 Remington caliber and a Universal M-1 .30 Carbine.

Law Enforcement Reaction

One result of Whitman's shooting rampage was that law enforcement agencies across the country began to develop counter sniper capabilities. Known as the "Dallas Clock Tower Shooting," the incident caused police agencies to consider their ability to stop a similar situation in the future. Virginia's State Police began an "Anti-Sniper" program in response. The modern "SWAT" or Special Weapons and Tactics concept, began in this era. My father, a Virginia state trooper, former competitive shooter and firearms instructor, became one of the first team members.

I vividly recall the anti-sniper rifle stored in a case inside my bedroom closet. The rifle had a variable 4 to 12 power Redfield scope for long range shooting. It fired a .243 Winchester cartridge manufactured by Federal, with a 90 grain bullet traveling through a heavy or "bull" barrel on a Winchester Model 70 bolt action rifle. Dad could consistently hit a softball size target at 500 yards with this rifle. Whitman's 6mm Remington and the .243 Winchester cartridges had many similarities, including same sized bullets. Fortunately, my father never had to fire the rifle in a practical situation, but he deployed several times in the late '60s and early '70s for executive protection duties, usually when the President or Vice President visited Virginia.

Political Assassinations

Members of the Nation of Islam murdered Malcolm X in New York City on February 21, 1965. Three men shot him twice with a sawed off double-barreled shotgun and 11 times with two pistols.

Martin Luther King lost his life on April 4, 1968 when James Earl Ray shot him from across a parking lot in Memphis, Tennessee while King was on his motel room balcony. The police found a Remington Model 760 pump rifle in .30-'06 that they assumed, but did not confirm, matched the bullets that killed King.

Sirhan Sirhan assassinated Robert F. Kennedy on June 5, 1968 in Los Angeles while Kennedy was on campaign as a candidate for the presidency. Sirhan, a Palestinian immigrant, shot him from close range with a .22 rimfire Iver Johnson Cadet revolver.

Political Response

Many Legislative and Executive Branch officials felt that they must "do something" about these shootings. The resulting laws became known as "gun control." The U.S. Treasury Department had proposed new laws related to commerce in firearms in 1965, partly in response to President Kennedy's assassination. The proposal, introduced as Senate Bill 1592 in March 1965, was not referred out of committee.

Democratic Senator Thomas J. Dodd of Connecticut introduced a similar bill in January 1967. A version of this law passed the Senate in May 1968 and the House the day after the Robert Kennedy assassination in June 1968. In October of that year, a revised version became the now well-known Gun Control Act of 1968.

John Kennedy's death had focused attention on firearms. The shootings of King and Robert Kennedy caused pressure on Congress at critical times in the legislative process to help the Act pass.[12]

1968 Gun Control Act

The 1968 Gun Control Act made it "unlawful" for any person to transfer any firearm or ammunition to a list of prohibited recipients, which included convicted felons, drug addicts, those adjudicated as mentally defective, anyone having been committed to a mental institution, illegal aliens and individuals dishonorably discharged from the Armed Forces.

Successful prosecution depended upon whether the transferring person knew or had reasonable cause to believe that the recipient was on the prohibited list.

Later additions to this list include a number of prohibitions against transferring firearms or ammunition to people under restraining orders for domestic abuse or convicted of a misdemeanor crime of domestic violence. Called "the Lautenberg Amendment," these provisions went into effect on September 30, 1996.[13]

The Act prohibits persons under the age of 18 years from possessing handguns or handgun ammunition and, with certain exceptions, prevents the sale of rifles or shotguns to those under 18 years of age and handguns to anyone less than 21. The Gun Control Act also mandates the licensing of individuals and companies engaged in the business of selling firearms. This provision stopped direct mail order of firearms by consumers. The Act outlaws the purchase of handguns by out of state residents, as well as stopping private sales between residents of two different states. The "paperwork" or forms to be completed upon transfer of firearms between licensed dealers and individuals originated with the 1968 Act.[14]

Proponents of the 1968 Gun Control Act might argue that had there been an equivalent law in effect in 1963 or 1966, it would have prohibited Lee Harvey Oswald from purchasing his rifle through the mail and, theoretically, would have kept Charles Whitman from purchasing firearms and ammunition at retail outlets because of his dishonorable discharge from the Marine Corps. However, it is doubtful that legal restrictions would have prevented these men from acquiring weapons in some other manner, especially since compliance with the law was dependent upon the purchasers' honesty in response to questions that determined their eligibility to purchase.

George Wallace

The next high profile shooting after passage of the 1968 Gun Control Act occurred when Arthur Bremer, a mentally ill 21 year old, shot Alabama Governor and former presidential candidate George Wallace twice with a .38 Special revolver. Bremer indicated in his diary that he sought fame and had no particular political motive, even though

Wallace had appeared in Laurel, Maryland as part of his presidential campaign when wounded by Bremer on May 15, 1972. No extremely high profile shootings after the attempted assassination of George Wallace occurred until the early 1980s.

John Lennon

A mentally ill young man named Mark David Chapman shot John Lennon in the back on December 8, 1980 as Lennon was entering his Manhattan apartment building in New York. Twenty-five-year-old Chapman had traveled from Hawaii to New York for the purpose of shooting Lennon. He used a small Charter Arms .38 Special revolver that held 5 rounds. Chapman emptied the gun at Lennon, hitting him four times. Doctors pronounced Lennon dead on arrival at a nearby hospital.

President Reagan

Ronald Reagan survived an assassination attempt by another criminally insane young man on March 30, 1981. John Hinckley, Jr. rode a bus from Dallas, Texas to Washington, D.C. for the express purpose of shooting Reagan. He used a cheap, R G Industries model RG-14, six shot .22 rimfire revolver to shoot at Reagan outside the Washington Hilton Hotel. Firing all six shots, Hinckley failed to hit the President directly, but the last bullet ricocheted off the side of the President's limousine and hit him under his left arm, grazing a rib and lodging in his lung.

Hinckley's aim had been spoiled by Secret Service agent Jerry Parr, who pushed Reagan into the limousine as the firing began. The first shot hit White House press secretary James Brady in the head and the second struck District of Columbia police officer Thomas Delahanty in the back of his neck. The third bullet did not hit anyone, but the fourth wounded Secret Service agent Tim McCarthy in the abdomen. The fifth projectile shattered on the bullet resistant glass of the limousine.

Hinckley had purchased the revolver at a Dallas pawn shop sometime prior to his attempt to kill Reagan. After finding him not guilty by reason of insanity at trial, the court incarcerated Hinckley in the St. Elizabeths Mental Hospital in Washington, D.C.

Firearms Owners Protection Act of 1986

Responding to allegations of wrongdoing by agents of the Bureau of Alcohol Tobacco and Firearms (ATF), seven years of bipartisan subcommittee hearings under the Senate Judiciary Committee investigated issues related to ATF violations of Second Amendment rights. The Senate Judiciary Committee determined that the 1968 Gun Control Act and ATF authority needed significant changes to protect civil rights. One committee report concluded that the proposed new laws would "...enhance vital protection of constitutional and civil liberties of those Americans who choose to exercise their Second Amendment right to keep and bear arms."[15]

Partly in response to Senate judiciary subcommittee reports, the Firearms Owners Protection Act of 1986 became law on May 19, 1986. (P.L.99-308, 1986) Also known as the FOPA, this Act prohibits registration of most firearms and their owners, clarifies the definition of prohibited persons under the Gun Control Act of 1968, and allows transport of firearms across states that prohibit their possession without prosecution, as long as the unloaded firearm and its ammunition are not immediately accessible.

An amendment to the Act froze the number of registered machine guns owned by private citizens. Therefore, all legally transferable machine guns under the National Firearms Act required registration with the ATF by May 19, 1986. Only licensed dealers with ATF approval, law enforcement, or the military, can now possess any machine guns registered after that date.

Brady Act

James Brady survived but suffered brain damage that left him with slurred speech and partial paralysis. He requires full time use of a wheelchair, and continues to have difficulty with mobility, speech, and cognitive function. Brady and his wife Sarah became active in the lobbying organization Handgun Control, Inc. The organization later changed its name to the "Brady Campaign to Prevent Gun Violence." Mr. and Mrs. Brady also founded the nonprofit Brady Center to Prevent Gun Violence. The Brady Handgun Violence Prevention Act, also known as the "Brady Act," passed in 1993, in large part as a result of their efforts.

The Brady Act requires performance of background checks on individuals prior to their purchase of firearms from a licensed dealer, unless an exception applies. Most of the prohibitions to prevent purchase had come about under the 1968 Gun Control Act. The new law, which went into effect on February 28, 1994 after President Bill Clinton signed it in 1993, requires approval by the National Instant Criminal Background Check System (NICS), maintained by the FBI or a State equivalent, prior to dealer sales of firearms. Transfers by private sellers not engaged in the business of dealing with firearms do not fall under the Brady Act. However, some states' laws require background checks for private transfers.

Stockton Shooting

A 26-year-old named Patrick Purdy opened fire on students at the Cleveland Elementary School in Stockton, California on January 17, 1989. Purdy used a Chinese-made semiautomatic AK-47 style, 7.62 x 39mm rifle to fire approximately 100 shots in about four minutes. Then he killed himself with a 9mm Taurus pistol. Five children, ages 6 to 9, died and 29 suffered wounds, along with one teacher.

Purdy had purchased both the rifle and pistol from licensed dealers and passed background checks. He bought the rifle on August 3, 1988 in Oregon and the pistol on December 28, 1988 in Stockton. Purdy had mental health issues, a criminal record, drug addictions, and alcoholism, but no crime conviction or adjudication of mental illness prevented him from passing firearms background checks.

California enacted America's first "assault weapons ban," largely in response to the Stockton shooting. The ban, known as the Roberti-Roos Assault Weapons Control Act, inspired the 1994 Federal ban, described below.[16]

Gun Battles: Ruby Ridge, Waco, and Oklahoma City

Possible violations of the National Firearms Act and the Firearms Owners Protection Act led to the deaths of multiple civilians and federal law enforcement officers at Ruby Ridge, Idaho and Waco, Texas in the early 1990s. These two events resulted in the killing of 84 civilians and five federal officers. Serious mistakes and overuse of force on both sides caused the deaths.

Timothy McVeigh and Terry Nichols claimed revenge against the federal government for its actions at Ruby Ridge and Waco as their motivation for bombing the Alfred P. Murrah Federal Building in downtown Oklahoma City on April 19, 1995. The bomb killed 168 people and injured over 680 more. The explosion destroyed or damaged over 200 buildings and 86 cars. McVeigh built a truck bomb using a rented truck, 5,000 pounds of fertilizer, 1,200 pounds of liquid motorcycle racing fuel and 16 gallons of diesel fuel. The resulting bomb had a blast equivalent to over 5,000 pounds of TNT.

101 California Street

Gian Luigi Ferri went into a law firm on the 34th floor of a building located at 101 California Street in San Francisco, California on July 1, 1993 and opened fire on its occupants. He used two 9 mm, TEC-9 handguns and a Chinese copy of the Colt 1911 .45 pistol. Ferri killed 8 people and wounded 6 others before committing suicide as the police closed in. The reason for the shooting never became clear, although Ferri appears to have suffered from mental illness.

The Ferri shooting, also called the "101 California Street Shooting" spurred the founding of a number of organizations to promote more gun control legislation. These include the Legal Community Against Violence (www.leav.org) and the Jack Berman Advocacy Center (J.B.A.C.), which lobby and organize with other groups in an effort to promote gun control and so, hopefully, reduce violence.

Federal Assault Weapons Ban

The Violent Crime Control and Law Enforcement Act of 1994, more commonly known as the Federal Assault Weapons Ban, became law when signed by President Clinton on September 13, 1994.[17] Among other provisions, this Act classified certain semi-automatic firearms as "assault weapons." It also banned "large capacity ammunition feeding devices" or magazines with a capacity of more than 10 rounds. The definition of assault weapon in the Act did not fit the longtime technical definition of an assault rifle. This new legal category frequently causes misunderstanding and arguments between gun control opponents and advocates, each of whom has a different understanding of the term.

A later chapter includes the full definitions of assault rifles and assault weapons.

The Assault Weapons Ban listed a number of arms by specific models, as well as enumerating features which created a prohibited class of assault weapons within the definition of the Act. The ban required any semi-automatic rifle that accepted a detachable magazine to have no more than one of the following features: folding or telescoping stock, pistol grip, grenade launcher, bayonet mount, flash suppressor, or threaded barrel designed to allow attaching a flash suppressor.

Manufacturers simply changed designs to eliminate banned features and produced "post-ban" versions that complied with the law. These post-ban rifles functioned identically to the pre-ban versions and accepted the high capacity magazines, legally grandfathered by the law and existing in great numbers. Most firearms experts considered the Act's provisions on these subjects as something of a joke.

The Act's definition of semi-automatic pistols and semi-automatic shotguns that violated the ban had even less effect on function.[18] The Federal Assault Weapons Ban prohibited by name the standard civilian version of America's service rifle, the Colt AR-15.

Columbine

On April 20, 1999, two mentally ill high school students, Eric Harris and Dylan Klebold, walked into Columbine High School in Columbine, an unincorporated area in Jefferson County, Colorado, and shot 36 people, killing thirteen and then themselves. Harris and Klebold had planned their attack for nearly a year. They constructed homemade bombs and illegally acquired firearms, black powder, and ammunition as part of their plan. The pair brought 99 improvised bombs made from propane tanks, pipes, gasoline and other flammables to the school.

In addition to the 99 homemade explosive devices, they had arrived at Columbine High School with a Savage 67H 12 gauge pump shotgun, a Stevens 311D 12 gauge double-barreled shotgun, a Hi-Point Model 995 carbine in 9mm, a TEC-YDC 9mm handgun, and 4 knives. They attempted to blow up the school cafeteria with propane bombs while hundreds of students ate lunch. Fortunately, the bombs failed to explode. Harris and Klebold then ran through the school and across the school grounds shooting people for approximately 45 minutes before killing themselves. Both had committed numerous felonies under state and federal laws prior to arriving at the school and beginning their massacre.

The shooters acquired their weapons through straw purchases. A friend, Robyn Anderson, bought the Hi-Point carbine and the shotguns for them at a Tanner gun show in Denver, Colorado during December 1998. Another friend, Phillip Duran, bought the TEC 9mm for $50.00 from a man named Mark Manes.

The motivation behind the Columbine Massacre remains uncertain. Both young men had problems with the law and mental illness issues. One took Luvox for depression. They had a deep interest in violent video games, and other students at the school did not find either of them socially acceptable.

Partly in response to the Columbine shootings, many police departments implemented a specific protocol for dealing with "active shooters," differentiated from the protocol to be followed in a hostage situation. Taught in Federal Advanced Law Enforcement Rapid Response Training (ALERRT) and similar courses, the tactics call for immediate movement towards the shooter to neutralize him as soon as possible before he kills or injures more victims. This response probably prevented even worse results at numerous shootings, including Virginia Tech in 2007 and the Washington Navy Yard in 2013.[19]

Wakefield, Massachusetts

Michael McDermott walked into his place of employment at Edgewater Technology in Wakefield, Massachusetts on December 26, 2000 and killed seven of his co-workers. He used a 12 gauge Winchester Model 1300 shotgun, an AK-47 style semi-automatic rifle and a .32 caliber semi-automatic pistol. McDermott seemed mentally ill, claiming he had traveled back in time to kill Nazis and Hitler, but the judge found him competent to stand trial. The court convicted him of seven counts of first degree murder, and imposed a sentence of seven consecutive life sentences without the possibility of parole.

This type of workplace shooting has become known as "going postal." The term derives from a string of five events at U.S. Post Office facilities from 1986 to 1993. A number of postal employees killed several co-workers while in violent rages. The killings usually involved guns, but one man killed his former supervisor with a sword and another ran over his boss with a car.

Beltway Sniper

A series of shootings took place during three weeks in October, 2002 at several locations throughout the Washington, D.C. area and along Interstate 95 in Virginia. Ten people died and three others suffered critical wounds. John Allen Muhammad and Lee Boyd Malvo, a minor, used a 1990 Chevrolet Caprice and a Bushmaster BM-15 rifle in .223 Remington to conduct their shooting rampage. The Caprice had the back seat removed so that Muhammad could crawl into the trunk and fire the rifle through a hole cut in the sheet metal near the license plate.

Muhammad and Malvo would park near a parking lot, gas station, or other public place, then shoot someone and drive away. They began their crime spree with murders and robberies in Louisiana and Alabama during August and September of 2002. Neither Muhammad nor Malvo could legally possess a rifle. Muhammad had a conviction of domestic violence on his record and Malvo had not reached the age of 18.

John Muhammad apparently had an interest in causing terror on behalf of Islamic jihad as his motivation for the shootings. Lee Malvo followed Muhammad's lead throughout the events. Both received multiple murder convictions in Virginia and Maryland. Virginia executed John Allen Muhammad on November 10, 2009. Malvo is serving a number of consecutive life sentences without the possibility of parole.

The Ban Expires

The 1994 Assault Weapons Ban expired on March 2, 2004. Since then, six attempts to renew the ban and strengthen its provisions have failed. Representative Carolyn McCarthy, a Democrat from New York, introduced a bill that would have renewed the Ban for an additional 10 years and defined more firearms as assault weapons. She introduced this bill in 2003, prior to expiration of the original law, and again in 2005 and 2007. The attempts did not survive the judiciary committee to have a floor vote. Mark Kirk, Republican representative from Illinois, also introduced a bill to reinstate the ban for 10 years and expand the list of assault weapons. His bill also died in committee.

Senator Diane Feinstein, Democrat from California, has attempted to extend and expand the Assault Weapons Ban twice. The first time was on March 2, 2004, when she attached an amendment to a statute called "Protection of Lawful Commerce and Arms Act," which prevented firearms manufacturers and dealers from having liability under civil suits for crimes committed with their products. This resulted in the Act failing the full vote in the Senate. That Act subsequently passed in 2005, without including renewal of the assault weapons ban.

Feinstein attempted again in early 2013 to renew the 1994 assault weapons ban and greatly increase its scope. The Senate Judiciary Committee approved a version of the bill strictly along party lines, with Democrats in favor and Republicans opposed, on March 14, 2013. Another chapter will cover the details of the bill, amendments, and voting by the full Senate.

President-elect Barack Obama, immediately after his November 4, 2008 election, included "making the expired Federal Assault Weapons Ban permanent" on his planned agenda as President.[20] He posted this statement on his campaign website and again on the Administration website[21] after his Inauguration. Attorney General Eric Holder repeated the Administration's desire to reinstate the Assault Weapons Ban during a February 25, 2009 press conference.[22]

Virginia Tech

Seung-Hui Cho, a mentally ill and disaffected student at Virginia Tech, shot 49 people with two handguns on April 16, 2007. He stalked his victims throughout the classrooms with a Glock Model 19 9mm and a Walther .22 rimfire pistol until the police arrived and he committed suicide. Cho had legally purchased both handguns, passing the required background check for each.

D.C. v. Heller

The United States Supreme Court overturned a Washington, D.C. ban on handguns in the case of *D.C. v. Heller* in 2008. This case confirmed the right to have a firearm for individual self- defense under the Second Amendment to the Constitution. While many historians and Second

Amendment scholars had always considered self-defense one reason for the Second Amendment, others disagreed. The *Heller* case officially put that disagreement to rest, at least for a while.

Binghamton, New York

On April 3, 2009, a mentally disturbed naturalized citizen from Vietnam named Jiverly Wong went into the Binghamton, New York American Civic Association building and shot 17 people before killing himself. Wong shot 99 times, 88 rounds from a 9mm Beretta 92FS and 11 from a .45 caliber Beretta TX4 Storm, both semi-automatic handguns. One of the guns had been legally purchased and registered by Wong in Broome County, New York, and the other in Englewood, California.

Fort Hood

A few months later, on November 5, 2009, U.S. Army Major Nidal Hasan broke Fort Hood post regulations by bringing personal firearms inside the gates, where he proceeded to shoot 45 people. Hasan fired all of the shots from an FN 5.7mm semi-automatic pistol. He also carried, but did not fire, a Smith & Wesson .357 Magnum revolver. Claiming jihad and an act of war on behalf of the Taliban, Hasan killed 13 and wounded 32 American soldiers or their family members. A Fort Hood post police officer, Sergeant Mark Todd, stopped him, shooting five shots with his service pistol. Three of the shots hit Hasan, rendering him a paraplegic. He has received a death sentence after his court-martial and convictions. At this writing, Hasan awaits execution in a military prison.

Gabrielle Giffords

United States Congresswoman Gabrielle Giffords (D – Arizona) suffered severe wounds when she was shot in the head on January 8, 2011 by Jared Loughner. He shot her with a 9mm Glock Model 19 semi-automatic pistol, then killed six people and wounded another 13 before bystanders stopped him. When he tried to reload his Glock, he dropped the loaded magazine on the sidewalk. One bystander grabbed the magazine while another hit Loughner on the head with a folding chair. Others tackled Loughner and subdued him.

A federal judge found Loughner incompetent to stand trial on two occasions, and then finally ruled him competent. He pleaded guilty to 19 counts and currently serves a life sentence in prison.

His pistol had been legally purchased at a retail store with the required federal background check a few weeks prior to the shooting. Loughner had used an extended magazine holding over 30 rounds. This event resulted in new calls for legal restrictions on the sale of high-capacity magazines to civilians.

Aurora, Colorado

Another criminally insane young man named James Holmes walked into a theater in Aurora, Colorado on July 20, 2012, carrying gas canisters and four firearms. Wearing body armor, he began firing into the audience, first with a 12 gauge Remington Model 870 shotgun and then with a Smith & Wesson M&P 15 semi-automatic rifle in .223, fitted with a 100 round drum magazine. The drum malfunctioned after approximately 45 rounds, at which point he opened fire with his Glock Model 22 .40 caliber handgun.

Twelve people died and another 58 suffered wounds from the gunfire. Holmes also booby trapped his apartment with homemade grenades and gasoline. When police arrived at the apartment, they disarmed the explosive devices. Holmes also carried, but never fired, a second Glock Model 22. Calls for more gun control increased in response to Holmes' actions. Sales of guns also jumped, primarily due to fears about an impending increase in gun control measures.

Oikos University

Seven students of Oikos University, a Korean Christian college in Oakland, California, lost their lives on April 2, 2012, when a former student named One Goh shot them with a .45 caliber semi-automatic pistol. Goh, a naturalized citizen from South Korea, who also wounded 3 other students, suffered mental illness and has not been tried due to a finding of lack of competency to stand trial. The pistol used had 10 round magazines and appears to have been acquired legally.

Newtown, Connecticut

The worst school shooting in American history took place in the Sandy Hook Elementary School at Newtown, Connecticut on December 14, 2012, when an obviously insane 20-year-old Adam Lanza, armed with a Bushmaster XM15 (same as an AR-15) and several extra magazines, shot the glass out of a large window, walked into the school, and opened fire.

Earlier that morning, Lanza had murdered his mother, who had worked at the school, with a .22 rimfire rifle. She was the legal owner of the XM15 rifle he used. Lanza took it and some of her other firearms to Sandy Hook, where he killed 26 people, mostly young children, and wounded two others. As police arrived he shot and killed himself with a pistol. The Bushmaster rifle he used met the requirements of Connecticut's existing assault weapons ban. This shooting caused a massive public discussion of gun control, of issues with the mentally ill, and of ways to prevent similar massacres in the future.

Boston Marathon

On April 15, 2013, two American citizens sympathetic to the agenda of Islamic terrorists exploded two improvised bombs made from pressure cookers during the Boston Marathon. Following the bombing, they shot two police officers, killing one, and remained at large for a period of time, after which one was killed in a gun battle with police and the other captured. Like Nidal Hasan at Fort Hood, brothers Dzhokar and Tamerian Tsarnaev seemed to believe that they acted on behalf of Islam in a religious war with the U.S.

Washington, D.C. Navy Yard

A mentally ill employee of one of the government contractors working at the Washington Navy Yard shot 15 people on September 16, 2013. Twelve of the shooting victims died.

The shooter, Aaron Alexis, had passed a background check and legally purchased the 12 gauge Remington 870 pump shotgun used in the shooting. He had 24 buckshot shells for the shotgun. Alexis took a 9mm service pistol from a security officer he had wounded and also used it to fire at people inside and outside the Navy office building. Law enforcement personnel shot and killed Alexis about 30 minutes after he had fired his first shot.

Crime and Passion

Separate from high profile shootings, acts of violence with weapons, including firearms, take place daily. Professional criminals, urban gang members, neighborhood robbers and others have used guns to wound and kill for many years. Much of this violence has its roots in the drug trade, although it has many causes, including the passions of domestic disputes.

Fights over children, fidelity, or property during marital break-ups seem to cause a form of insanity in some people. While at least temporarily insane, they may have access to weapons and, if their insanity includes violent tendencies, the distraught sometimes wound or kill their former partner or themselves.

These examples of "gun violence," from everyday urban street crime to ultra-high profile mass shootings and assassinations, lie at the foundation of the fears many Americans have about guns in America. Modern communications, especially cable TV and the Internet, often place graphic visual and audio details of violent events in nearly everyone's home. These stories can run repeatedly for many days, weeks and sometimes even months.

Reactions to Violence

Obviously, everyone finds these acts appalling. The divide occurs in the methods by which different people choose to try to reduce the number and severity of the crimes. Two basic and very different trends have become apparent in reaction to crime and shooting events. The first involves both citizens and law enforcement working toward the ability to actively defend against violence and safely secure guns. The second embraces political efforts to pass more laws in attempts to reduce access to firearms or to impose new rules to lower the effectiveness of the weapons used. This second trend now goes by the name "gun violence prevention."

The idea of gun violence prevention causes many politicians, with the support of large numbers of their constituents, to propose and sometimes enact laws to restrict ownership of firearms by everyone. By the very nature of attempts to prevent violent acts by legal means, these laws paint with a very broad brush. They would restrict ownership for all citizens in an effort to stop wrongdoing by a few. Some of this group sincerely believe that total civilian disarmament would best protect Americans from misuse of guns. They would rely upon the police to have sole responsibility for the safety of individual citizens.

Conclusion

Gun control advocates frequently clash with citizens who want to own guns for possible defense of themselves and their communities. This latter group buys more guns and ammunition, takes classes on the use of weapons, applies for concealed carry permits, and plans for active measures to stop violence themselves. These people believe, with legal and historical justification, that their right to keep and bear arms for self and community defense lies at the core of the Second Amendment. They take responsibility for their own safety and for the safety of their families. They also fear, and sometimes even despise, anyone who wants to take away what they see as their right to have the ability to defend themselves.

The gun control approach to violence would lower the numbers of guns, put more limits on who can own guns, and reduce the power of guns available to civilians, all through more laws. The often bitter conflict that results from these polar opposite reactions seems likely to continue for the foreseeable future, creating a national crisis over gun control. The next chapter explains the desire of "pro-gun" citizens to stay armed.

Chapter 2

FEAR OF VIOLENCE

Legal Prevention and Physical Protection

Violence and Law

The American system has always punished criminals for the misuse of firearms. Stronger punishment for using weapons illegally appears to have caused the crime rate in the United States, including the gun homicide rate, to drop by over half since 1980.[1] Unfortunately, severe punishment does not always work to deter assassinations and random mass shootings. A substantial number of organizations, politicians and others point to these incidents as reasons we should have laws that restrict or prevent possession of firearms by many, if not all, American civilians.

Proposed Federal laws to create new crimes follow the strict liability standard of intent for punishment. In other words, if law enforcement finds someone possessing the outlawed items, the intent for possession has no relevance because the possession itself constitutes the crime. Of course, law enforcement and military personnel exemptions would apply, at least while carrying out their duties. Those in favor of disarming everyone in an effort to prevent others from being killed or wounded by firearms have a number of names. Most recently, they have called themselves "gun violence prevention activists" or "advocates of gun violence prevention." Those opposed to such laws have given the advocates less flattering labels such as "gun grabbers" and "anti-gunners." Anti-gun theory argues that laws which prevent or reduce possession of firearms by the population in general will translate to prevention or reduction of the criminal use of firearms.

One "irony" of gun control occurs when efforts to restrict firearms or reduce the type available for purchase cause increased sales of both guns and ammunition.

Moral Authority

Some gun control opponents ascribe more sinister motives to the proponents of gun restrictions. They claim that many bureaucrats, politicians and organizations have the broader goal of increasing the power of government relative to the power of individual citizens. Some point to attempts to disarm citizens, combined with a simultaneous increase in the power of law enforcement weaponry as evidence.[2] "The war on drugs and, more recently, post-9/11 antiterrorism efforts have created a new figure on the U. S. scene: the warrior cop – armed to the teeth, ready to deal harshly with targeted wrongdoers, and a growing threat to familiar American liberties."[3]

Both sides in this debate claim moral authority. Both also attack the other side with name-calling and allegations of treason, insensitivity to violence, and the violation of citizens' rights.

Those who would restrict access to firearms in an effort to reduce violence assert that they do so in an effort to reduce the number of people killed or injured. They also suggest their "pro-gun" opposition does not care about victims of violence, and some even refer to them as insurrectionists, in response to their talk about the Second Amendment allowing the people to protect themselves against a tyrannical government.[4]

Josh Horowitz, executive director of the Coalition to Stop Gun Violence, coined the concept of opposing gun control as an insurrectionist idea in his book, *Guns, Democracy, and the Insurrectionist Idea.* He states that people claim they need weapons in order to fight their own government.

Guns and Money

Another argument, made by gun control advocates, accuses the NRA and firearms manufacturers and other members of the "gun industry" of having money as their motivation for opposing stricter gun laws. This assertion has apparently resonated with some, at least on Wall Street. Pension funds and institutional investors feel pressure to dump their holdings in firearms makers. Many investors have given in to this pressure. Wall Street calls this sort of investment, subject to institutional bias, a "vice stock" or "sin stock." However, some investors have found that these stocks present good value as a result of the depressed prices derived from a lower demand.[5]

J. P. Morgan may stop doing business with firearms makers as part of its efforts to distance itself from relationships viewed as risky to its reputation. The bank may stop lending to gun companies in light of the massacre of children in Newtown, Connecticut.[6]

In fairness, the principals on both sides of the debate do stand to benefit financially. Members of the pro-gun lobby (firearms manufacturers, dealers, and the NRA) benefit via the inflated prices for products for which there is the potential for scarcity should restrictive laws be passed and, in the case of the NRA, increased membership. Members of the anti-gun movement reap an increase in donations from like-minded supporters.

The conflict over firearms law supports dozens if not hundreds of groups on both sides of the argument. Thousands of people receive substantial salaries and benefits as employees of organizations that advocate one side or the other. It is easy to see why a person might see financial motivation on the part of everyone involved, especially after viewing the solicitations for contributions from all of these organizations.

Anti-Gun Organizations

The groups promoting more and stricter laws in response to the misuse of guns include a large number of non-governmental organizations, the current Executive Branch of the United States government, most of the Democratic Party, and most of the mainstream media. The Coalition to Stop Gun Violence serves as an umbrella for 38 national organizations. These groups call themselves "National Gun Violence Prevention Organizations."[7] According to its mission statement, the CSGV "seeks to secure freedom from gun violence through research, strategic engagement and effective policy advocacies."[8]

The organizations take positions ranging from relatively moderate advocacy of background checks at gun shows and improving the national instant background check system to ideas as extreme as complete and total civilian disarmament. Comments from politicians, activists and media include the statement that "we have to do away with guns."[9] A statement from former New York Police Commissioner Patrick

Murphy says, "the time has come for us to disarm the individual citizen."[10] Fox News contributor Juan Williams said in a January 17, 2000, Boston Globe opinion piece, "We should be talking about getting rid of the guns in this country."[11] The Brady Center to Prevent Gun Violence seeks to eliminate all handguns, even for the purpose of self-defense. One of its officials, Nelson "Pete" Shields, III makes it clear that the Brady Center hopes to gradually eliminate handguns "one step at a time" to reach its ultimate goal.[12]

Other anti-gun organizations include the Center for Gun Policy and Research at Johns Hopkins University, the Brookings Institution, The Third Way, The Violence Policy Center, Organizing for Action (President Obama's former campaign) and many others.

Former New York City mayor Michael Bloomberg has funded an organization called "Mayors Against Illegal Guns" to lobby for legislation that restricts access to firearms. This organization has a large public presence as well as millions of dollars for running ad campaigns and pressuring lawmakers. It spent 12 million dollars on a campaign to put pressure on U.S. Senators in an attempt to influence their vote on the gun control bill proposed in April of 2013.[13] Elements of the Executive Branch of the Federal government have always supported increased gun control, but President Barack Obama has taken this support to an entirely new level. He has promised "to use the full force of his office to enact gun-control measures."[14]

President Obama posted his thoughts about "gun violence" on the White House website early in 2013. The language points to a need to better protect children and communities from mass shootings. He then goes on to propose "common-sense steps we can take right now."[15] He published a plan called "Now is the Time" on January 16, 2013. It calls for background checks for all gun sales, bans on "assault weapons" and high capacity magazines, as well as restrictions on "armor-piercing" ammunition, additional import restrictions, and a number of other measures. It also includes funding gun violence research, increasing the flow of mental health information from health professionals to law enforcement and encouraging more safe storage of guns. The full plan can be found at www.whitehouse.gov/issues/preventing-gun-violence.

Along with President Obama, most of the Democratic Party and its leadership appear firmly on the side of regulating firearms in an effort to inhibit mass shootings and reduce gun violence. These include Vice President Biden and Senate Majority Leader Harry Reid. With some exceptions, the Democratic Party at every level of the government has become known for supporting more gun control.

Many in the television media have strongly endorsed stricter gun laws and advocated actively on their behalf. For example, CNN, MSNBC and CBS have clear bias in favor of these laws. Fox News, on the other hand, leans toward the right of center, although its commentators appear to have no objections to background checks or gun registration. Even prime-time TV dramas often present an anti-gun violence message that sometimes veers toward advocacy of gun control. Generally speaking, television provides a major platform for anti-gun spokespersons.

For several years, a previously unheard of level of resources has been poured into this issue, with a substantial increase in 2013, largely as a result of the Sandy Hook Elementary School shootings in Newtown, Connecticut. Travel expense alone must exceed millions of dollars as the President has visited various communities around the country in an effort to pressure lawmakers. Reporters follow along or make separate trips to interview various people involved, spending more millions. Mayor Bloomberg has spent tens of millions of dollars and the Coalition to Stop Gun Violence, along with its members, have spent even more. In addition to the money, the time and effort expended have been astronomical.

Anti-gun organizations have proposed a number of ideas in addition to those put forth by President Obama in an effort to reduce the illegal use of guns. While they continue to promote a Federal assault weapons ban and a Federal universal background check system, the organizations have a wish list of other proposals. The list is available on the website www.csgv.org, and advocates will entreat state governments to adopt these ideas for new laws. One involves developing a new mental health standard focused on the "dangerousness" of the patient rather than an adjudication of whether he or she meets current mental standards for legal ability to possess firearms.[16] Another idea proposes legal liability for gun makers and other members of the "gun industry" for the misuse of firearms by criminals.

The CSGV website also mentions "counter marketing," which involves large cities or states with significant law enforcement buying power to pressure the industry for concessions. These organizations oppose "concealed carry" for self-defense and will lobby states, as well as the Federal government, against reciprocity and against more liberal concealed carry laws. They also want manufacturers to "micro stamp" bolt faces so that empty cartridge cases will have an identifier to trace the casing to the gun that fired it. In theory, this will allow law enforcement to then trace the ownership of the gun to find the shooter.

On February 26, 2012 in Sanford, Florida, George Zimmerman fired a 9mm bullet from a Keltec PF9 semi-automatic pistol into the chest of Trayvon Martin. The Keltec had a 7 round magazine and Zimmerman legally carried it under Florida law. The long and public trial of Mr. Zimmerman for homicide resulted in a "not guilty" verdict. Florida's self-defense law required Zimmerman to have a "reasonable fear of imminent great bodily harm or death" in order to use lethal force for defense. The jury apparently believed that Trayvon Martin beat Mr. Zimmerman's head on the sidewalk in an effort to gravely injure or kill him. Because of that belief Mr. Zimmerman walked away a free man.

The Federal government has not completed its investigation of possible violation of the civil rights of Trayvon Martin by Mr. Zimmerman's actions. So far no evidence of suspicious facts that would support a civil rights prosecution has come forth. (Forensic Lab Report, March 8, 2012, by Amy Fiemert, Florida Department of Law Enforcement) Partly in response to the killing of Trayvon Martin by George Zimmerman, the National Gun Violence Prevention Organizations have begun to oppose stand your ground laws like the one in Florida. The Zimmerman case did not include a stand your ground law issue, but these laws have been promoted by the NRA.

A stand your ground provision allows someone threatened or attacked to immediately use deadly force in defense when in fear of imminent bodily harm or death. Many states require an effort to retreat or otherwise avoid a confrontation before allowing lethal force in self-defense. Organizations opposed to these laws call them "shoot first" laws or "kill at will" laws and lobby for their rejection or repeal.

Other anti-gun proposals include bans on various types of guns and magazines, registering all firearms, limiting the number of firearms any one person can own and restricting types and amounts of ammunition legally possessed. Possible taxes on guns and ammunition, as well as insurance requirements, have been considered. Some states have considered complete bans of firearms or handguns, but the Supreme Court has overturned total ban statutes in Washington, D.C. and Chicago. (More on proposals, bans, and politics in later chapters)

Fear of Violence and Active Self-Defense

While Federal and state law has increased gun control under different acts between 1968 and 2004, a large portion of the United States population has reacted to violence in a very different way. Called "gun nuts" and worse by gun control advocates, these "pro-gun" or "pro-Second Amendment" citizens respond to threats of violence with preparation for self-defense. In what seems a more traditionalist or conservative point of view, these Americans have supported expanded concealed or open carry laws and increased authority for self-defense in the home. They oppose many or all proposals they consider anti-gun. These people see having a firearm as the most effective and probably only realistic way to stop an armed criminal or insane person. They argue that the amount of time it takes for police to respond to a call about an active shooter gives him time to shoot many victims before law enforcement ever arrives.

Americans who favor having guns for defense of themselves and their communities have continued to purchase firearms, accessories, and ammunition in large quantities. Accessories include magazines for the guns in question. For semi-automatic handguns, the standard capacity of these magazines generally ranges from seven or eight rounds to 16 or 17 rounds per magazine. A modern civilian version of a service rifle typically uses either 20 or 30 round magazines. The AR-15 with the 30 round magazine probably holds the position as the most popular rifle in America.

The Second Amendment, to people who understand guns and history, means the ability to defend their families and their communities from threats of violence, regardless of the source. This group would protect those they care about by the most efficient means possible, usually a semi-automatic rifle of the AR-15 type in today's world. Often having military experience, people of this mindset believe that there is the very real possibility that they might have to defend their families and communities from some form of attack. They don't want to be victims or rely on the belated response of government officials to guarantee the safety of their families and neighbors.

Very few pro-Second Amendment Americans believe they will somehow battle the United States government with their rifles. They know that the discussion of defense or response to tyranny would involve a response to a failed constitutional government or invader, not to a duly-elected democratic government functioning under the American system.

Treason

The advocates of armed self-defense and community defense or "gun rights" sometimes also consider their opponents to be committing treason, and they see any attempt to disarm people as a violation of the Second Amendment. In the eyes of people who would respond to violence by stopping it themselves, this violation threatens the safety of families and communities. One particularly outspoken opponent of gun control, named Aaron Hawkins, stated in a YouTube video,[17] "Any Congress person or Senator who puts their name to any law which infringes on the right to bear arms should be arrested for treason."[18] While this viewpoint may seem to be extremist, it is reflective of the concerns of quite a few gun owners, many of whom would be considered centrists.

Government employees' and elected officials' oaths of office, modeled after the one set out in the Constitution for the President, state in part: "I do solemnly swear (or affirm) that I will ... to the best of my ability, preserve, protect and defend the Constitution of the United States." While it would be unfair to categorize all elected officials who support gun control as traitors, many of the gun control proposals under consideration actually do infringe upon the Constitutional right to own and carry firearms. It is because of this incongruity that many Second Amendment advocates and citizens may correctly accuse office holders who vote for these proposals of violating their oaths.

Pro-gun Organizations

Name-calling and accusations of treason aside, pro-gun America also has a huge organizational structure lobbying against gun control and for the right to bear arms. Led by the National Rifle Association (NRA), the organizations are as numerous as the "anti-violence" organizations. They include the Citizens Committee for the Right to Keep and Bear Arms, the Second Amendment Coalition, the Second Amendment Foundation, Gun Owners of America, The National Association for Gun Rights, Guns Across America, the National Shooting Sports Foundation, and many, many others. The financial resources, as well as time and effort put into defending the right to bear arms, probably match the resources expended to oppose ownership of firearms in America.

Americans who resist efforts to restrict or reduce their rights to have firearms want the ability to defend themselves, their families and communities against unexpected violence. They fear local criminal activity, random mass shootings, terrorism, the breakdown of law and order due to war or disaster, and other potential threats of violence. The emotional objections to any reduction in individual defense capabilities is borne in the country's long history of self-reliance. Some citizens also fear a failure of Constitutional government that would require citizens to take up arms in order to restore a representative system.

Crime and Mass Shootings

U.S. crime rates have declined considerably in the last 30 years, but concerns about violent criminals continue in many parts of the country.[19] Random mass shootings, on the other hand, have increased steadily since the 1980s, with 18 in the 1980s, 54 in the 1990s, and 87 in the 2000s.[20] Law enforcement has defined "active shooters" as "criminals who attempted to murder people in a confined area, where there are lots of people, and who chose at least some victims randomly."[21]

The U.S. Secret Service, in collaboration with the Department of Education, conducted a "National Threat Assessment" to aid in prevention of school-based attacks.[22] In reference to stopping an attack, their assessment found: "Despite prompt law enforcement responses, most attacks were stopped by means other than law enforcement intervention."[23] The short duration of the attacks explains the inability of law enforcement to stop them. "Close to half of the incidents were known to last for 15 minutes or less from the beginning of the shooting to the time the attacker was apprehended, surrendered or stopped shooting. One-quarter of the incidents were over within five minutes of their inception."[24] Whether through intuition, training, experience, or other factors, Americans understand that time matters during a violent attack. Practically speaking, only the ability to stop a shooter bears more critically on the situation than does time.

"The problem is that by the time the police arrive, lots of people are already dead. So when armed citizens are on the scene, many lives are saved. The media rarely mention the mass murders that were thwarted by armed citizens..."[25]

Home Invasion

Another type of criminal attack people fear, called "home invasion," occurs all too often in America. Law enforcement defines these attacks as "forceful entry into an occupied dwelling with violent criminal intent." For example, two men named Steven Hayes and Joshua Komisarjevsky invaded a Connecticut home on July 23, 2007. They found William Petit sitting on a couch on his front porch, where they clubbed him to unconsciousness with a baseball bat, then bound him in his basement.

Next, the invaders captured and bound Mr. Petit's wife, Jennifer, and two daughters, Hayley, 17 and Michaela, 11. The men had targeted them at a store and followed them home. Hayes forced Jennifer to go to her bank and withdraw $15,000, then raped her and strangled her to death. Komisarjevsky sexually assaulted Michaela. Petit awoke, escaped, and went to a neighbor's house for help. Before the police intervened, the invaders had doused Jennifer's body and the girls with gasoline and set the house on fire, killing the girls. The police eventually caught both men. They were caught, tried, and convicted of capital murder, and then sentenced to death. Although Connecticut repealed the death penalty in 2012, their sentences stand, and both remain on death row as of 2014.

News of the Petit home invasion caused gun sales to dramatically increase in Connecticut. Similar events across the nation contribute to citizens keeping firearms for self-defense.

Many Americans simply do not believe that regulating firearms will solve mass shootings or the broader problem of violent crime. Instead, they believe in the need, and the right, to protect their families and themselves with the best weapons they can afford. Those who would reduce the effectiveness or availability of guns for responsible ownership cause those who assume responsibility for their own safety to feel massive resentment, if not fear. The fear comes from the very real possibility that the means to stop a violent attack will itself become illegal.

War in the Future

Many also fear government restrictions will prevent them from acting individually or collectively to defend their homes and restore order to their communities in the aftermath of nuclear war. "For decades, a group of physicians has been urging other clinicians, political leaders and the public to imagine an event of apocalyptic proportions that could very possibly occur today."[26] Quoting Dr. Victor Sidel, co-founder of International Physicians for the Prevention of Nuclear War (IPPNW), JAMA says: "The acquisition of nuclear weapons by nations in addition to the United States ... the Soviet Union, the United Kingdom, France, China, Israel, India, Pakistan and North Korea ... increases the risk of their being used."[27]

The Arms Control Association (ACA) estimates that the world has 9,730 nuclear warheads.[28] The U.S. has 5,100, Russia 3,500, France 300, China 240 and the U.K. 225. (Id.) India, Pakistan and Israel have unknown numbers of warheads, but ACA assumes each country holds 100. (Id.) "North Korea has separated enough plutonium for roughly 4 - 8 nuclear weapons."[29]

A Department of Defense Task Force recently reported:

> *The actual or threatened acquisition of nuclear weapons by more actors, for a range of different reasons, is emerging in numbers not seen since the first two decades of the Cold War. Many of these actors are hostile to the U.S. and its allies, and they do not appear to be bound by established norms or deterred by traditional means. In some cases of established nuclear powers, nuclear forces are seen as the most affordable and effective alternative to deter superior conventional forces; i.e., nuclear weapons are viewed as a legitimate war fighting capability, especially if their vital domestic or*

regional security interests are threatened. For example, Russia has publicly stated in doctrine and backed it up with training and exercises that they will use theater nuclear forces if necessary to deter aggression against the homeland. (cites omitted)

The pathways to proliferation are expanding. Networks of cooperation among countries that would otherwise have little reason to do so, such as the A.Q. Khan network or the Syria-North Korea and Iran-North Korea collaborations, cannot be considered isolated events. Moreover, the growth in nuclear power worldwide offers more opportunity for 'leakage' and/or hiding small programs, especially since current resources to support safeguards are already strained and will be increasingly challenged by cases of noncompliance.

In short, for the first time since the early decades of the nuclear era, the nation needs to be equally concerned about both 'vertical' proliferation (the increase in capabilities of existing nuclear states) and "horizontal" proliferation (an increase in the number of states and non-state actors possessing or attempting to possess nuclear weapons).[30]

Local devastation from nuclear war does not require an attack on America. "Recent research by Dr. Ira Helfand shows that limited use of nuclear weapons, such as a nuclear exchange between India and Pakistan, could cause widespread crop failure and worldwide famine."[31] In other words, the radioactive dust clouds from ground burst nuclear explosions would endanger Americans, regardless of where the explosions occur.

The unpredictability of war continues in modern times. "The tide of war is receding, except where it isn't."[32] China could go to war with Japan over islands in the East China Sea or with Taiwan (Formosa) to force its return. Pakistan and India harbor longstanding animosities and regularly experience conflicts along their long common border. Israel and Iran might clash at any moment. Iran's government publicly endorses constant hate-filled excoriations of Israel. North Korea vocally threatens both South Korea and the United States.

The Defense Intelligence Agency concluded that the Democratic People's Republic of Korea (North Korea) has the ability to send a nuclear armed intercontinental ballistic missile (ICBM) to the United States. North Korea has successfully tested nuclear warheads three times since 2006 and recently put a satellite into orbit, demonstrating that it possesses the basic technological ability for delivery. A single nuclear detonation above North America would cause a catastrophic electromagnetic pulse (EMP) that would cause a long-lasting electricity blackout. "An EMP attack would collapse the electric grid and other infrastructure that depends on it – communications, transportation, banking, finance, food and water – necessary to sustain modern civilization and the lives of 300 million Americans."[33]

Iran, a country where huge crowds chant "Death to America," may soon have nuclear weapons and ICBMs. Its president states: "Saying 'Death to America' is easy. We need to express 'Death to America' with action. Saying it is easy."[34] "The Pentagon reports that Iran could flight test an intercontinental ballistic missile capable of reaching the U.S. by 2015."[35] Iran has defied the U.N. Security Council and multiple U.N. sanctions in its effort to become a nuclear power.

Iran appears to have negotiated away some of its nuclear weapons-making capabilities recently, in return for reduced sanctions. However, many observers, especially the Israelis, do not believe that Iran will halt its efforts to acquire an atomic bomb.

Many see having safety equipment, and the skill to use it, as a duty to uphold. This duty includes protecting family, community, and the nation from threats of any kind. These people see firearms as a necessary part of their equipment. They agree with Mark Helprin when he discusses Israel's defense. "Though history may never repeat itself exactly, it does have affection for certain themes. One of these is that of a nation suicidally disarming because it rests upon the laurels of the past, or believes in the satisfying delusion that by intellectual formulation it can safely predict the future intentions and capabilities of rivals and enemies."[36] Those who would remain well armed see the effort to "prevent violence" with firearms regulation as a naive belief of the moment that does nothing to address real threats.

Terrorism

Iran also supports terrorist organizations that oppose what Iranians call "the Arrogance," by which it means the United States, Israel, and their allies. Hezbollah, Hamas and possibly al Qaeda receive moral and material support from Iran. Terrorists have already attacked the U.S. with hijacked aircraft, truck bombs, improvised bombs (like the pressure cookers in Boston) and firearms. No one can predict what they will use next in the effort to punish or undermine the United States. There seems a real danger that terrorists could acquire and use nuclear weapons. People who would continue to bear arms want to retain the capability of defending their communities against the lawlessness that could result in the aftermath of a major terrorist attack.

The U.S. has reduced the ranks of al Qaeda since 9/11, but the terrorist organization has not admitted defeat. "While al Qaeda's central leadership may be weakened, the rest of the group has morphed into smaller entities and dispersed, which has made the threat harder to predict and track."[37] "The group was never close to being extinguished. It adapted."[38] Al Qaeda also seems "as determined as ever to attack the West."[39] The Islamic State of Iraq and Syria, or ISIS, threatens attacks on U.S. soil, using the hashtag "Calamity Will Befall U.S. to lay out its plans.

"These terror groups have thrived. So despite all the successes in the war on terror, al Qaeda has maintained a steady stream of new recruits, replacing the members that have been killed or captured by the U.S."[40] Those "who endorse Osama bin Laden's jihadist message inevitably move on to the global war against the West."[41] So the need to defend against terrorists appears as real as ever. Many Americans prefer the option to provide their own defense, rather than having to cower in their homes, "sheltering in place," while waiting for law enforcement to act.

Terrorists manage to acquire or improvise weapons no matter what the legal prohibitions. France has some very strict firearms regulations, yet an Islamic terrorist managed to acquire nine guns, including fully automatic sub-machineguns. Mohammed Merah killed four French soldiers in two separate attacks on March 11 and March 15, 2013. Then, on March 19, he attacked a Jewish school, murdering one adult and three children. Merah told a French TV editor that the killings were necessary "to uphold the honor of Islam."

Mohammed Merah used the same Colt .45 1911 semi-automatic pistol to shoot all of his victims. This model normally has a seven shot magazine. The other guns found at his apartment included an AK-47, UZI, STEN, Winchester 12 gauge pump, Colt Python, a Glock 9mm and two more .45 1911 pistols. A police sniper killed him when he fired one of the submachine guns at the officers who came to arrest him on March 22, 2013.

Terrorists attack with improvised explosive devices (IEDs) almost daily in the Middle East. America suffered one of these attacks on April 15, 2013 at the Boston Marathon, with bombs made from pressure cookers. Terrorists also use knives or other bladed weapons.

In May 2013, two Islamist terrorists used knives and a cleaver to kill a British soldier named Lee Rigby near the Royal Artillery barracks in Woolwich, England. A London suburb, Woolwich hosted the Olympic shooting events a few months earlier. Shouting "Allah Akbar" (God is great), the killers slashed Lee Rigby to death in front of several onlookers. No one present had the ability to stop the killing, arguably because of England's highly restrictive laws on gun ownership and possession.

A day after the Boston bombing, on April 16, an unknown group executed an apparently well planned attack on an electrical substation in California.[42] It was considered an act of domestic terrorism... "one former Federal regulator is calling it a terrorist act that, if it were widely replicated across the country, could take down the U.S. electric grid and black out much of the country."[43] The attack disabled 17 large transformers and took the substation out of service for 27 days.[44] A coordinated terrorist attack could cause nationwide major power outages for weeks or even months in a man-made disaster that would likely result in looting, break-ins, and other crime.

Disaster Aftermath

In addition to concerns about criminals, mentally ill mass shooters, war, and terrorism, Americans worry that they may need to defend against lawlessness following a disaster. "Accidents (nuclear), earthquakes, tsunamis, and terrorist attacks all pose risks of widespread devastation."[45]

Law and order have broken down in the past for areas as large as a major city and could easily do so again. Los Angeles experienced overwhelming riots after the Rodney King verdict in 1992. Over 20,000 police, California National Guard and Federal Troops took six days to restore order. Hurricane Katrina had a similar effect on New Orleans in 2005. Incidents of looting and other crimes skyrocketed and continued for weeks. Local police, who had also suffered devastation from the storm, were unable to function.

Regardless of the cause, when civilized behavior fails and families face threats of violent attacks, many Americans want the means to stop those threats immediately themselves. They know that lacking those means, the time it takes for "first responders" to arrive can and will allow the attackers to succeed.

Fear of Oppression

Americans also fear the violence of oppression or tyranny. This concept lies at the core of the Constitution's Second Amendment, and does not seem to be well understood by either side in today's gun control debate. It consists of the idea that all capable, competent citizens can and will act collectively to resist any attempt to destroy or overthrow our Constitutional government.

This concept came to America with the English as they settled the Colonies in the 17th and 18th centuries. Writing in his *Commentaries on the Laws of England*, Sir William Blackstone discusses..."the principal absolute rights which appertain to every Englishman. But in vain would these rights be declared, ascertained and protected by the dead letter of the law. [The law] has therefore established certain other auxiliary subordinate rights of the subject, which serve principally as barriers to protect and maintain inviolate the three great and primary rights of personal security, personal liberty, and private property."[46]

The auxiliary rights included "that of having arms."[47] This right acknowledged "the natural right of resistance and self-preservation, when the sanctions of society and laws are found insufficient to restrain the violence of oppression."[48] The chapter closes with the statement that "to vindicate these rights, when actually violated or attacked, the subjects of England are entitled...to the right of having and using arms for self-preservation and defense."[49]

During the drafting of the Constitution, its framers, who had full awareness of the rights Blackstone explained, discussed tyranny and oppression, as well as how to prevent both. Speaking of the right to bear arms, one of the framers asked: "But what is tyranny? Or how can a free people be deprived of their liberties? Tyranny is the exercise of some power over a man, which is not warranted by law, or necessary for the public safety. A people can never be deprived of their liberties, while they retain in their own hands, a power superior to any other power in the state."[50]

Discussing military force as a source of power in government, Mr. Webster, one of the leading founders of the United States, goes on to say:

> *Before a standing army can rule, the people must be disarmed; as they are in almost every kingdom in Europe. The supreme power in America cannot enforce unjust laws by the sword; because the whole body of the people are armed, and constitute a force superior to any band of regular troops that can be, on any pretense, raised in the United States. A military force, at the Command of Congress, can execute no laws, but such as the people perceive to be just and constitutional; for they will possess the power and jealousy will instantly inspire the inclination, to resist the execution of a law which appears to them unjust and oppressive.*[51]

The *Connecticut Courant* (a Hartford newspaper) put it this way in 1788: "It is a capital circumstance in favor of our liberty, that the people themselves are the military power of our country. In countries under arbitrary government, the people oppressed and dispirited, neither possess arms nor know how to use them. Tyrants never feel secure, until they have disarmed the people."[52]

Originally, the tyranny feared came from European monarchies, one of which (England) saw defeat by Americans immediately prior to the drafting and ratification of the Constitution and Bill of Rights. We needed to "keep and bear arms" for defense against possible combinations of citizens and foreign powers who might try to take over the country.

Armed citizens stood ready to defend against invasion or any threat to their freedom. "For a people who are free, and who mean to remain so, a well-organized and armed militia is their best security."[53]

Alexander Hamilton writing as "Publius" in The Federalist XXIV warned of possible threats to the new country:

Though a wide ocean separates the United States from Europe; yet there are various considerations that warn us against an excess of confidence or security. On one side of us and stretching far into our rear are growing settlements subject to the dominion of Britain. On the other side and extending to meet the British settlements are colonies and establishments subject to the dominion of Spain. This situation and the vicinity of the West-India islands belonging to these two powers create between them, in respect to their American possessions, and in relation to us, a common interest. The savage tribes on our Western frontier ought to be regarded as our natural enemies and their natural allies; because they have most to fear from us and most to hope from them. The improvements in the art of navigation have, as to the facility of communication, rendered distant nations in a great measure, neighbors, Britain and Spain are among the principal maritime powers of Europe. A future concert of views between these nations ought not to be regarded as improbable – The increasing remoteness of consanguinity is every day diminishing the force of the family-compact between France and Spain. And politicians have ever with great reason considered the ties of blood as feeble and precarious links of political connection. These circumstances combined admonish us not to be too sanguine in considering ourselves as entirely out of the reach of danger.[54]

Hamilton correctly predicted most of America's 19th century wars. We fought Britain again (1812-1814), Spain's Mexican Colony (1842) and Spain itself (1898). War with the "savage tribes" continued for most of that century.

Wars and Rumors of War

Destruction of our government by foreign powers and depredations by terrorists continue as risks today. The countries that maintain or seek nuclear weapons could use them against us. The prospect of invasion or massive attack faced America several times in the 20th century and, in theory, could again.

German efforts to encourage and assist Mexico with an invasion of the United States in 1916 helped cause our entry into World War I. Mexico rejected the German proposal, known as the Zimmerman message, but not until after considering the unlikelihood of its success.

The Axis powers of World War II planned to rule the world, if the Allies had not stopped them by 1945. Japan (Ni-Go and F-Go Projects) and Germany (Uranprojekt) had nuclear weapons programs and worked on methods to deliver them in North America. Germany had designed and begun work on both intercontinental bombers (Ju 390) and long range ballistic missiles (V2/A-10). The Germans pioneered the concept of submarine launched ballistic missiles, with the idea of striking America.[55] The Japanese designed and began to build huge submarine aircraft carriers as part of their efforts to bomb America.[56]

The most recent threat of destruction of the United States came from the Soviet Union. The standoff between it and the U.S. during the 1962 Cuban Missile Crisis almost resulted in an unimaginable nuclear war.

Since then, the U.S. and the Soviets have nearly fired nuclear missiles at each other four times. "The Cuban missile crisis is the best-known example of narrowly avoiding nuclear war. However, there are at least four other less well-known incidents in which the superpowers geared up for nuclear annihilation. Those incidents differed from the Cuban missile crisis in a significant way. They occurred when either the U.S. or Russian leaders had to respond to false alarms from nuclear warning systems that malfunctioned or misinterpreted benign events."[57]

These near disasters happened on November 9, 1979; June 3, 1980; September 26, 1983; and January 25, 1995. An error in judgment by military officers would have resulted in a nuclear launch on each of those dates.[58] Unfortunately, experts believe that similar mistakes will continue to occur. "Complex organizations relying on even more complex machinery can find new and unexpected ways to fail. In fact, a comprehensive study of nuclear accidents has shown convincing historical evidence that, despite measures taken to prevent them, such accidents are inevitable."[59]

Violence of Tyranny

Regardless of foreign threats, some American citizens have serious concerns about modern threats of oppression from domestic sources. This other aspect of the "violence of tyranny" contemplates the failure of our Constitutional government due to internal sources rather than attack or invasion. State, local, and Federal governments seem to violate the Constitution repeatedly in modern times, especially the Bill of Rights. Usually done in the name of public safety or national security, the violations accelerated after the terrorist attacks of 9/11/2001.

Even election campaigns by incumbents may have involved unconstitutional use of government power to seek advantage over opposition, in defiance of the First Amendment. The IRS, the Federal Election Commission (FEC), and other Federal agencies appear to some to have attempted to thwart the efforts of conservatives in elections with an organized campaign "to chill conservative donors and groups via the threat of government investigation and prosecution."[60]

In an apparent attempt to suppress free speech, "beginning in March, 2010, the IRS engaged in an unprecedented campaign of harassment against conservative groups, either through denials in approving their tax-exempt-status applications, or through endless and burdensome audits.[61] When called upon to account for its actions by Congressional investigators, the IRS claims to have irretrievably "lost" all of the relevant emails from seven different computers.

The Justice Department falsely accused Fox News reporter James Rosen of committing a crime in order to establish grounds for a search warrant to access his email accounts and telephone records. This action clearly violated the Privacy Protection Act, Supreme Court precedent and the First Amendment.[62] The government also improperly acquired Associated Press reporters' electronic communications without notice or court approval, claiming the need for a criminal investigation.

With the collection of electronic communications and related information of American citizens inside the United States by the National Security Agency (NSA), some say the country has become a "massive surveillance state."[63] Peggy Noonan of the *Wall Street Journal* makes it clear that, in addition to Fourth Amendment issues of unreasonable searches and appropriate probable cause, the use of modern technology to read or listen to private communication infringes upon the public's assurance of free speech protected by the First Amendment. Knowing that what they say risks retribution from government, Americans will become careful about what they say, constricting their freedom of expression.[64]

Many people are of the opinion that President Obama, a former Constitutional law professor himself, currently leads the effort to circumvent or reinterpret the Constitution. A Georgetown Constitutional law professor, Nicholas Rosenkranz says that Mr. Obama "flouted the Constitution" when he suspended parts of laws without Congressional approval.[65]

With the announced intention to change the national character, the Administration and its supporters have placed the full force of their resources behind changing the Second Amendment. Knowing that outright repeal cannot succeed, this effort focuses on action by all three branches of government to reinterpret its meaning.

Yet none of these government actions equate to the "violence of tyranny" by an unconstitutional government. Almost everyone involved can lose their job after the next election (except Federal judges). The impeachment process can function if the people insist upon its use, not only for elected officials, but also for judges.

Further amendment of the Constitution could also allow for the clarification or reassertion of rights.

Anyone who believes that the Second Amendment allows citizens to throw out a democratically elected government by force of arms does not understand history or the Amendment. Only an unconstitutional government can fit the definition of tyranny that warrants overthrow. For example, some future leader could declare martial law, suspend elections, and attempt to dissolve Congress. Actions like that could not stand against the will of the people, as long as they continue to keep and bear arms.

Conclusion

Fear of violence with firearms has caused a tremendous "anti-gun" effort to restrict or eliminate access to guns by American citizens in an effort to prevent violence. Equally strong fears of all types of violence fuel the need to oppose anti-gun efforts so that Americans can continue to have weapons for self-preservation and community defense. Both the current administration in Washington, D.C. and international forces seek severe restrictions or elimination of small arms in the hands of U.S. citizens. At the same time, many Americans fiercely stand on their core Constitutional rights to have weapons and defend themselves. They resist civilian disarmament efforts with great determination. The next chapter addresses the politics resulting from this continuing conflict.

Chapter 3

GUN VIOLENCE POLITICS

International Pressures and the Continued Fight Over Guns

After Sandy Hook

America reacted with horror and dismay after the December 2012 shooting rampage by mentally ill, 20 year old Adam Lanza. He used a stolen, "Post-Ban" Bushmaster XM15 to kill 26 people, mostly six year old first graders, at Sandy Hook Elementary School in Newtown, Connecticut.

Nancy Lanza, Adam's mother, owned all of the guns involved and had taken him to ranges, where he learned to shoot. Known as an "avid gamer," he practiced combat shooting skills with video games. Some of these games, like "Call of Duty," resemble combat simulation programs used by the military.

Lanza shot and killed his mother with a bolt action .22 rimfire rifle, then took her XM15, a 12 gauge shotgun and a Glock 10mm semi-automatic pistol to the school. The shotgun stayed in the car, and he committed suicide with the Glock before police arrived.

The reaction to Sandy Hook included far more than emotion. The tragedy and its aftermath stayed in the headlines for months, until the Boston Marathon bombing on April 15, 2013. Gun control organizations flourished, coordinating their efforts to influence lawmakers at every level of government. "It's this political infrastructure that has grown out of this tragedy in part that is going to force people to do the right thing," according to Senator Chris Murphy (D., Conn.) referring to the unprecedented combination of groups advocating national gun control.[1]

Gun Control "Playbook"

Drafted in late 2011 to early 2012, prior to Sandy Hook, an 80 page guide to messaging for gun control advocates became available. Called the "Gun Control Playbook" by some, "Preventing Gun Violence Through Effective Messaging," by Frank O'Brien and others, the playbook provides guidance for organizations and individual "spokespeople" to promote gun control. It also goes by the name "The Guide."

This Guide says, "DON'T talk about 'gun control.' DO talk about 'preventing gun violence'."[2] It acts as a tool for "advocacy around gun violence prevention" and begins with the premise that "laws matter because, if they're strong enough, they can keep people alive."[3] The Guide provides ideas, strategies and tactics for influencing lawmakers, in part through their constituents, to pass stronger (not stricter) laws "to protect people from gun violence."[4]

The Guide explains how to promote repeal of Stand Your Ground (so-called "Shoot First") laws, how to enact universal background checks for every gun sold,[5] and how to oppose concealed carry reciprocity.[6] It also describes how its readers can encourage "Banning the sale of assault weapons and high capacity ammunition magazines."[7]

The Guide has a section on how to use media attention from "High-Profile Gun Violence Incidents" to push for more laws.[8] "A high-profile gun violence incident temporarily draws more people into the conversation about gun violence."[9] "That means we should seek out opportunities to engage these newly accessible audiences – through mainstream media appearances, online outreach, and other channels."[10]

The guide suggests seeking long-term relationships after a shooting event. "In terms of building support, our goal at moments such as this should be to make a connection with someone that will be sustainable after the individual incident fades from memory."[11]

Advice from this Guide appears to have been followed by many gun control advocates after Sandy Hook, quite successfully in many states. "Despite Congress' inability to enact even a compromise background-check bill, however, Newtown did more for the gun control movement than any other event in decades, prompting a flood of new legislation in state capitals."[12]

Connecticut passed one of the most far reaching gun control laws in the country. Called "An Act Concerning Gun Violence Prevention and Children's Safety" or Connecticut Senate Bill No. 1160, the law prohibits sales of magazines holding over ten rounds, expands the definition of an assault rifle, expands the list of banned assault weapons, and requires all sales to include a background check. It also requires government issued certificates for purchases of both firearms and ammunition.

Colorado passed a similar bill, with a 15 round limit for magazines and requiring background checks for all sales. The law's passage "raised hopes among supporters of tougher restrictions that lawmakers in Washington and states across the country would soon follow suit."[13] Maryland, New York, Delaware, Rhode Island, and New Jersey also passed new, stricter bans and requirements. Washington, D.C., California, and Hawaii already had bans and other gun control measures in place. The California State Assembly recently passed 17 more restrictions. However, Governor Jerry Brown vetoed seven of the measures as overreaching or unnecessary. California already had some of the strictest gun control laws in the U.S.

Confiscation and Mental Health

Gun confiscation by law enforcement has begun in at least three states. "In recent months, the sheriff of Cook County, Illinois, which includes Chicago, launched a gun confiscation program; California began adding agents assigned to take away firearms; and New York enacted a law that paves the way for such a program."[14] Called the Armed Prohibited Persons System (APPS), Special Agents of the California Bureau of Firearms use information on gun ownership to target gun owners without a search warrant or court order. "Officials in Illinois and California can systematically confiscate firearms because they collect more data on gun owners than most states, experts said. They merge data on who owns guns with a list of people who can't legally do so, whether because of a felony conviction, violent misdemeanor, restraining order, involuntary stay in a mental hospital, or court adjudication that they are mentally unstable."[15]

This activity concerns gun advocates in the context of background checks. The data collected during transfers could find its way to Federal gun seizure units charged with collecting, for example, assault weapons or large capacity magazines, if the more extreme anti-gun forces have success in the future. While they did not pass, both the universal background check and the large capacity magazine ban amendments in the 2013 Senate Gun Control Bill received over 50 votes.

A common thread of severe, violent mental illness runs through most, if not all, of the mass shootings in recent history. Some people suggest improving mental-health treatment and strengthening civil-commitment laws as a response.[16] Others would focus on laws to prohibit possession of firearms by anyone deemed mentally ill, without a judicial ruling.

Current Federal law requires an adjudication of dangerousness or incompetence to manage affairs "which includes a determination by a court, board, commission, or other lawful authority" to prohibit receiving firearms. It also calls for prohibiting those committed to a mental institution from having guns.[17] Several groups advocate expanding this definition to include far more people. The Department of Justice has proposed a new regulation to include anyone required to receive outpatient mental health treatment as a prohibited person.[18]

Some states have passed laws to allow officials to take guns away from anyone mental-health professionals report as dangerous, without any adjudication. "New York lawmakers this year passed sweeping gun-control legislation that creates a statewide database of handgun owners that will allow authorities to see if any are prohibited from possessing guns. The law also requires mental health professionals to report if patients are dangerous, and authorizes law enforcement to confiscate those patients' firearms. Officials said that the new data and authority will help law enforcement confiscate more guns there."[19] California Attorney General Kamala Harris urges the Obama administration "to consider a similar federal gun-confiscation program."[20]

Push Back

Pro-gun laws also increased after Sandy Hook, either in response to the shooting or in reaction to anti-gun efforts. "This year, five states have passed seven laws that strengthen gun restrictions, while 10 states have passed 17 laws that weaken them, according to the Law Center to Prevent Gun Violence, which tracks and promotes gun-control laws."[21] Many of the new laws make it easier for citizens to carry concealed weapons. Some increase the number of places where people can legally carry concealed weapons, and others ease or even eliminate the permit process. "States have passed more measures expanding rather than restricting the right to carry firearms."[22]

"22 states have passed laws that limit property owner's ability to ban firearms in vehicles in parking areas."[23] Called "Bring Your Gun to Work" laws by opponents, they require employers to allow employees to leave firearms in their vehicles during work hours.

The laws have the purpose of protecting the rights of workers to have guns for self-defense during commutes. Some employers worry that an angry employee will "go postal," grab a gun, and come back shooting. Other employers respect their employees' desire to have firearms in vehicles and support the parking lot laws.[24]

Several states, including Virginia, made records related to concealed carry permits confidential.[25] Illinois, long one of the strictest gun-control states, lifted its ban on concealed weapons. "A bill to allow concealed carry passed each of the state's two legislative houses [on July 9, 2013] by more than a three-fifths vote, overriding a veto [the week before] by Democratic Gov. Pat Quinn. This law epitomizes the conviction in much of the U.S. that access to firearms offers the best protection against crime."[26] Many have the same feeling about defending against a mass shooter in public. "The problem is that by the time the police arrive, lots of people are already dead. So when armed citizens are on the scene, many lives are saved."[27]

The sentiment that defenders must meet force with force shows again in laws related to school security and protecting children. Efforts include staff training, physical measures and security plans. However, Sandy Hook Elementary School had a state-of-the-art physical security system and Connecticut an "assault weapons" ban. Adam Lanza simply shot his way in and killed the unarmed adults who tried to stop him. The obvious need to stop a shooter immediately has resulted in the placement of more members of law enforcement, known as resource officers, in schools and, in some states, armed school staff.

Resource officers spend their shifts at schools as an on-site guard and resource for other purposes. Additional state and Federal funds for more of these officers have become available since Sandy Hook. Several states have considered or implemented allowing qualified staff to have firearms at schools. Indiana, South Dakota and Texas, among others, either allow or require trained, armed staff members on school campuses.[28] Texas calls its law along these lines the "Protection of Children Act" and South Dakota passed the "School Sentinel" bill.[29]

"Parchment Barriers," or written laws, simply do not deter everyone from violence. Either due to mental illness, apathy, or fanaticism, some people will kill others without regard to rules or fear of consequences. Gun control advocates hope that laws restricting firearms purchases or prohibiting possession will prevent at least some violence. "Bans are intended to decrease the availability of certain types of firearms to potential offenders, and thus reduce the capacity of such offenders to perpetrate crime," according to the *American Journal of Medicine* in reference to restrictions on assault weapons, high-capacity magazines and some types of ammunition.[30]

In theory, firearms laws could act as one means to prevent violence and complement law enforcement.[31] The review of firearms law in the *Journal of Medicine* concludes that "available evidence is insufficient to determine the effectiveness or ineffectiveness on violent outcomes of banning the acquisition and possession of firearms."[32] The possibility or probability that someone bent on violence will find another weapon if his first choice becomes unavailable contributes to the uncertainty about whether gun laws can or will prevent violence.

Called the "Substitution Effect," this concern acknowledges that denying a violent person the use of a firearm could result in his using a knife, a machete, Molotov cocktail, an improvised bomb or some other weapon to wound or kill.[33] Serious people with the responsibility to protect children and others realize that they cannot rely upon laws to stop violent people. Thus the focus on having at least one trained, armed "protector" in schools and elsewhere.

2013 Senate Gun Control Bill

The President used the full force of his office to support gun control legislation initiated in the U.S. Senate. Senator Dianne Feinstein (D-California) introduced a new, more restrictive Federal assault weapons ban in January of 2013. Named the Assault Weapons Ban of 2013, the bill would have prohibited the sale and transfer of most semi-auto center fire rifles and their magazines.

The Senate Judiciary Committee approved a version of new gun legislation that did not include Feinstein's proposal on March 14, 2013. The revised bill focused on straw purchases, mental health measures, school safety, and universal background check provisions. A straw purchase refers to a buyer who purports to buy a firearm for his or her own use, but who actually does so on behalf of another, possibly prohibited, purchaser. Senate Majority Leader Harry Reid pledged to allow amendments, including the Feinstein bans, when the new bill reached the Senate floor. Senate Democrats from gun-friendly states helped cause the bans to fail before leaving Committee. These included Mark Begich (Alaska), Mark Pryor (Arkansas), Mary Landrieu (Louisiana), Max Baucus (Montana), Kay Hagan (North Carolina) and Heidi Heitkamp (North Dakota).

The background check provisions of the revised bill, proposed by Senator Charles Schumer (D., N.Y.) faced serious resistance, and Senate leaders hoped to replace it with a bi-partisan version.[34] The bi-partisan concept, called the "Toomey-Manchin Compromise" reworded Schumer's proposed law in an attempt to draft a measure acceptable to the full Senate.

The administration and gun-control community pulled out all of the stops to promote passage of the Senate bill. The bill and proposed amendments, one of which restored the Feinstein bans, would reach the Senate floor for votes in mid-April. "Advocates for tougher gun laws, led by New York City Mayor Michael Bloomberg, have started to run television ads in recent weeks to pressure Republicans and Democrats alike to back the broader bill before Mr. Reid brings it to the Senate floor."[35] President Obama held campaign-style events around the country in an effort to spur movement in Congress. He traveled to Colorado on April 3 and Connecticut on April 8 to meet with local leaders and encourage them to push lawmakers.[36]

"Organizing for Action, the advocacy group launched by several of the president's campaign advisors, [tried] to rally support for gun-control legislation ahead of the Senate debate. OFA [teamed] up with Mayors Against Illegal Guns to hold events April 13 across the nation."[37]

A Democratic think tank organization called "The Third Way" worked with the families of victims of Adam Lanza to form an organization called "Sandy Hook Promise." It helped lead the effort to advocate for the background check legislation. A group of gun control proponents known as "Americans for Gun Safety" helped found The Third Way in 2005. Sandy Hook Promise families knew that background checks would not have mattered for them in the Newtown shooting.[38] The purchase of the rifle there had included a background check, and had also been in full compliance with Connecticut's assault weapons ban.

"Lawmakers also heard from gun-control advocates [on April 9], including relatives of those killed in the mass shooting at Sandy Hook Elementary School, who arrived at the capitol to press for a bill that could reduce gun violence. About a dozen family members of Newtown victims traveled with President Barack Obama on Air Force One Monday evening [April 8] after the President spoke in Hartford, Conn."[39]

The Senate voted on five of the amendments to the Gun-Control Bill on April 17. Majority Leader Reid could have brought the background check amendment to the floor for an up or down vote, with 51 votes needed for passage. But this would have opened the bill to 30 hours of debate and to the inclusion of pro-gun amendments unacceptable to him and the President.

"The White House demanded, and Mr. Reid agreed, that Congress should try to pass the amendment without such a debate."[40] Senator Reid then used the unanimous consent rules to allow voting on nine amendments, each requiring at least 60 votes to succeed. The Senate added a tenth proposed amendment on the day of the vote.

Texas Senator John Cornyn's amendment to implement national concealed carry reciprocity received 57 favorable votes, including 13 Democrats. Under the unanimous consent rules, it failed by three votes. This would have required every state to recognize every other state's concealed-carry permits.

The large capacity magazine ban amendment brought 54 "yes" votes and 46 "no" votes (including 10 "no" votes from Democrats). The assault weapons ban failed 40 to 60, with 15 Democrats opposed. The extra (tenth) amendment offered by Wyoming Senator John Barrasso to protect gun ownership privacy passed 67 to 30.

The Toomey-Manchin Compromise background check amendment failed at 54 to 46. Obviously, it would have passed if not for the "unanimous consent" method of voting. Four Democratic Senators from the states of Arkansas, Alaska, North Dakota, and Montana opposed the amendment and voted "no." Four Republicans voted in favor: Susan Collins (Maine), John McCain (Arizona), Pat Toomey (Pennsylvania) and Mark Kirk (Illinois). The alternate Republican background check amendment also failed, 52 to 48. The remaining amendments did not have a vote because the Majority Leader pulled the bill. It included the Democrats' version of background checks, which probably would not have passed. The mental health, straw purchase, and school safety provisions might have passed, but the real purpose of the bill had failed. Senator Reid voted "no" to the background check amendment so that he could meet the procedural requirement for bringing it back later. The bill and amendments can be reintroduced if 60 Senators vote to do so.

Vice President Biden announced the vote results with the reaction: "This is far from over. This is far from over."[41] Majority Leader Reid said: "I want everyone to understand this is just the beginning, not the end."[42]

After pulling the entire gun control bill from a vote, Harry Reid stated on the Senate floor: "I have spoken with the President. He and I agree that the best way to keep working toward passing a background check bill is to hit pause and freeze the background check bill where it is. But we should make no mistake; this debate is not over. In fact, this fight is just beginning."[43]

Referring to the compromise background check amendment after the vote, President Obama spoke from the White House Rose Garden with some of the Sandy Hook family members behind him. He blamed the failure of the bill to pass on three causes. First: "The gun lobby and its allies willfully lied about the bill." Second: The Senators who voted against it had "no coherent arguments as to why we wouldn't do this. It came down to politics." And finally, "a minority was able to block it from moving forward by this continuing distortion of Senate rules."

He also said, "And I see this as just round one ... We're going to have to change. ... I believe we're going to be able to get this done. Sooner or later, we're going to get this right."[44]

The alleged willful lie by the gun lobby relates to the fear that computer background checks would turn into a form of registration. "Mr. Obama is technically right that Manchin-Toomey would not create a federal firearms registry. Then again, its most clamorous supporters are also contemptuous of the Second Amendment, and they are explicitly hoping for a fifth Justice to overturn the Supreme Court's landmark gun-rights rulings. Manchin-Toomey opponents can be forgiven for worrying that gun controllers will attempt to build a registry from whatever records they get."[45]

"Banning certain types of semi-automatic rifles failed 40-60 with 15 Democrats opposed. Those 15 Democrats, along with numerous Republicans, are the true mainstream on guns in America: open to reasonable compromises as long as they safeguard individual rights."[46]

The Irony

Many Americans reacted to the gun control proposals by buying up guns and ammunition. Certain models of guns, the AR-15 and Glock pistols, for example, sold at record levels. Ammunition of many calibers sold out immediately, and continues to sell out as soon as it's delivered to retailers. Sometimes called "the irony of gun control," efforts to enact more restrictive laws seem to increase sales. Background checks for dealer sales rose from under one million for the month of January 2012 to over two million in January 2013, in response to the introduction of the Feinstein Gun Control bill and other post Sandy Hook proposals.[47]

Even in Newtown, as well as statewide in Connecticut, gun sales surged.[48] Reasons cited include citizens taking responsibility for keeping families safe, and concerns over future gun control restrictions.[49]

Partly in response to high profile shootings and news about new gun control, millions of Americans have secured the right to carry a concealed weapon in public. "Data gathered by the Kansas attorney general's office pointed to a probable doubling of concealed carry permits for the most recent fiscal year that ended June 30."[50] This trend exists across the nation, with Florida, Ohio, Oklahoma, Tennessee,

Wyoming, Texas, Utah and Wisconsin all reporting record numbers of applicants.[51] Alaska, Arizona and Wyoming recently joined Vermont in allowing citizens to carry concealed weapons without a permit.[52] "Applications for 'concealed carry' permits are soaring in many states, some of which recently eased permit requirements. The numbers are driven in part by concern that renewed gun-control efforts soon could constrain access to weapons, along with heightened interest in self-defense in the wake of mass killings in Newtown, Conn., and Aurora, Colo."[53]

The Future

Conflict over gun control laws appears inevitable for the foreseeable future, at the ballot box, in the courts, and in the media. "Neither side shows signs of budging, even an inch."[54] Matt Bennett of The Third Way calls the gun control effort "a long road" and expects the "gridlock" on gun policy to continue.[55]

The "actors within the gun violence prevention movement" seem to take every opportunity to follow the aforementioned "Messaging Guide." After the George Zimmerman verdict, President Obama read from a prepared statement: "We should ask ourselves if we're doing all we can to stem the tide of gun violence that claims too many lives across this country on a daily basis."[56] America should expect a massive media blitz, anti-gun lobbying effort and reintroduction of gun-control legislation whenever a shooting event provides more ammunition for the actors within the anti-gun movement.

Navy Yard

The media jumped on the Navy Yard shooting immediately after Aaron Alexis, using a pump shotgun, shot 20 people, killing 12 on September 16, 2013. Commentators almost instantly reported that Alexis used an AR-15 rifle and a Glock pistol. These incorrect reports followed the Messaging Guide's advice to take advantage of the spotlight before knowing the facts.

When the authorities made it clear that Aaron Alexis used a pump action 12 gauge Remington Model 870 shotgun, the media and anti-gun advocates fell silent. Purchase of the shotgun had included a background check. The handful of buckshot ammunition fired was a type that has served American citizens in some form for well over a century.

Absent several justifications for new calls to pass more gun laws, the focus shifted from the gun used to mental health.

However, many people will remember the news about an AR-15 and a Glock as if it were true. Once reported by the news, falsehoods often seem like facts in human memory. I never saw any retraction of the mistaken or intentionally wrong reports. The various media outlets supposedly made corrections via their websites, but nothing with visibility comparable to the original, erroneous reports.

The High-Profile "Pivot"

"High-profile gun violence incidents" attract media attention and elicit strong emotional response. "The truth is, the most powerful time to communicate is when concern and emotions are running at their peak."[57] "There is often a compelling case to be made for immediate action, pivoting from the emotion of a high-profile incident to calls for legislative action or specific policy changes."[58] "We need to use language where our message flows from the expression of concern into our broader argument. It can't be an abrupt pivot."[59]

President Obama provided an excellent example of the "pivot" during his remarks on gun violence on March 28, 2013. Speaking to the group "Moms Demand Action for Gun Sense in America," the President said in reference to his "common-sense proposals" and heartbreak: "Tears aren't enough. Expressions of sympathy aren't enough. Speeches aren't enough. We've cried enough. We've known enough heartbreak."[60] After saying that he did not propose taking away anybody's gun rights, he made the pivot: "And now's the time to turn the heartbreak into something real."[61]

Next, he implored his listeners to get involved and pressure Congress to pass the "common sense" laws on background checks, straw purchases, assault weapons bans and magazine capacities. However, none of these measures would have made any difference in Newtown, which provided the context for the speech.

The President made this pivot again quite clearly during his speech at the memorial service for those slain at the Navy Yard.[62] He said: "As President, I have now grieved with five American communities ripped apart by mass violence: Ft. Hood, Tucson, Aurora, Sandy Hook, and now the Washington Navy Yard. And these mass shootings occur against a backdrop of daily tragedies as an epidemic of gun violence tears apart communities across America, from the streets of Chicago to neighborhoods not far from here."[63] President Obama went on to talk about all of the individual Navy Yard victims, and then said:

> *These families have endured a shattering tragedy. It ought to be a shock to all of us, as a nation and as a people. It ought to obsess us. It ought to lead to some sort of transformation. That's what happened in other countries when they experienced similar tragedies. In the United Kingdom, in Australia, when just a single mass shooting occurred in those countries, they understood there was nothing ordinary about this kind of carnage. They endured great heartbreak, but they also mobilized and they changed. And mass shootings became a great rarity.*[64]

Later in the speech, after discussing the comments of one of the doctors who treated the Navy Yard victims, he continued:

> *But we Americans are not inherently a more violent people than folks are in other countries.. We're not inherently prone to mental health problems. The main difference that sets our nation apart, what makes us so susceptible to so many mass shootings is that we don't do enough, we don't take the basic common sense actions to keep guns out of the hands of criminals and dangerous people. What's different in America is it's easy to get your hand on a gun.*
>
> *And a lot of us know this. But the politics are different, as we saw again this spring. And that's sometimes where the resignation comes from – the sense that our politics are frozen and that nothing will change.*
>
> *Well, I cannot accept that. I do not accept that we cannot find a common sense way to preserve our traditions, including our basic Second Amendment freedoms and the rights of law abiding gun owners, while at the same time reducing the gun violence that unleashes so much mayhem on a regular basis.*
>
> *It may not happen tomorrow and it may not happen next week. It may not happen next month. But it will happen, because it's the change that we need. And it's a change overwhelmingly supported by the majority of Americans.*

By now, though, it should be clear that the change we need will not come from Washington, even when tragedy strikes Washington. Change will come the only way it has come, and that's from the American people.

So the question now is not whether as Americans we care in moments of tragedy. Clearly, we care. Our hearts are broken again. We care so deeply about these families. The question is do we care enough, do we care enough to keep standing up for the country that we know is possible even though it's hard and even if it's politically uncomfortable?

Do we care enough to sustain the passion and the pressure to make our communities safer and our country safer? Do we care enough to do everything we can to spare other families the pain that is felt here today?

Our tears are not enough. Our words and our prayers are not enough. If we really want to honor these 12 men and women, if we really want to be [a] country where we can go to work and go to school and walk our streets free from senseless violence without so many lives being stolen by a bullet from a gun, then we're going to have to change. We're going to have to change.[65]

This completes the pivot from concern and heartbreak to political agenda. And make no mistake: "Basic common sense actions" means universal background checks, assault weapons bans, and magazine capacity limits. None of these steps could have prevented the Navy Yard shooting, but the President asks Americans to "honor" the victims by "changing." He means far more than accepting the "common sense" actions currently proposed. He really means for America to disarm its civilian population, as Australia and the United Kingdom have done.

President Obama nominated Vivek Hallegere Murthy, M.D., as United States Surgeon General in late 2013. Dr. Murthy, president of the organization named Doctors for America, formerly Doctors for Obama, has supported a wide array of gun control policies. Pro-Second Amendment organizations oppose his confirmation because of concerns that Dr. Murthy will use the office of Surgeon General to further the administration's campaign against gun ownership.

The Senate Health, Education, Labor and Pensions Committee, chaired by Senator Tom Harkin, D - Iowa, voted to confirm Murthy on

February 27, 2014. As of this writing, it appears that the White House will probably delay the final confirmation vote until after the November 2014 election, in order to help Senate Democrats who would vote in favor keep their seats in pro-gun states.

Australia

The mention of Australia and the United Kingdom and their reactions to mass shootings has deep implications. On April 28 and 29 of 1996, a mentally ill 28 year old named Martin Bryant went on a shooting rampage in Australia. Bryant used a Colt AR-15 .223 and an FN/FAL 7.62 x 51mm, both semi-automatic rifles, to kill 35 and wound 23 people over that two day period. After a carjacking where he killed the car's occupants, police chased him to a standoff and capture. At trial, Martin Bryant received 35 life sentences, plus 1,035 years without parole, in the psychiatric wing of a prison in Tasmania.

Severe gun control resulted from Bryant's insanity. Australia banned semi-automatic rifles, semi-auto shotguns and pump shotguns.

United Kingdom

England had some of the strictest gun laws in the world by 2010. The United Kingdom (which includes England) had banned semi-auto rifles and shotguns, pump action guns, lever actions and all handguns. It allowed single and double-barreled shotguns for bird hunting and rimfire single shot or bolt action rifles to hunt small game. These required special licenses. Despite these laws, on June 2, 2010 in Cumbria, England, a 52-year-old taxi driver named Derrick Bird shot 23 people, killing 12, and then killed himself. Bird, licensed to have firearms, used a 12 gauge double barreled shotgun and a Czech made CZ-452 bolt action .22 rimfire to shoot his victims. The country reacted by banning all firearms.

When my wife, Kimberly, and I went to the Olympics in London in 2012 to watch the U.S. Olympic shooting team, we sat in very expensive temporary ranges. England apparently did not want to provide permanent ranges because it might encourage learning shooting skills. The country had to suspend its firearms laws for the Olympics to allow the .22 target rifles and pistols, clay pigeon shotguns and air pistols. Given his public statements such as those delivered at the Navy Yard

Memorial, it is easy to infer that President Obama wants us to have gun restrictions like those of the United Kingdom.

World Politics

The President's reference to Australia and the United Kingdom fuels the fear that the U.S. will give up its sovereignty to the U.N. or other international bodies that would attempt to impose unacceptable regulations, including domestic disarmament. This fear seems far-fetched, but may actually have sound foundations.

A group of people called "transnationalists" seek to impose their legal agenda without following the process of representative government.[66] This "legal transnationalism" movement wants U.N. officials to supplant elected representatives accountable to voters for domestic rule on a number of issues, including firearms ownership. " 'The idea that a U.N. official can sit in judgment of the U.S.' is one of its main innovations. Transnationalists want to...restrict gun rights and much more – all without having to win popular majorities or heed American constitutional limits. And these advocates are making major strides under an Obama administration that is itself a hotbed of transnational legal thinking."[67]

Transnationalists do not behave as secret conspirators, and clearly state their goals, as well as the methods to be used. "The preferred entry point for importing foreign norms into American law is the U.S. court system. Over the past two decades, activist judges have increasingly cited 'evolving' international standards to overturn state laws."[68] Another tactic involves avoiding the U.S. House of Representatives through aggressive promotion of international treaties, which require only Senate ratification.[69]

Small Arms Treaty

The United States voted in favor of a resolution adopting the Arms Trade Treaty in the U.N. General Assembly on April 2, 2013. Also called the Small Arms Treaty, the "United Nations Protocol Against the Illicit Manufacturing of and Trafficking in Firearms, their Parts and Components and Ammunition," its official title, has several provisions that affect private ownership.

Article 3 of the Protocol calls for "systemic tracking" of firearms, parts and ammunition "from manufacturer to purchaser."[70] Article 7, "Record Keeping," sets out a comprehensive monitoring system. A U.N. organization named the "Coordinating Action on Small Arms" (CASA) will develop rules, called International Small Arms Control Standards (ISACS). They include controls over the access of civilians to small arms. Article 6, "Confiscation, Seizure and Disposal," calls for authorities to seize and destroy firearms considered "illicitly trafficked."

Secretary of State Kerry signed the treaty on behalf of the United States on September 25, 2013, shortly after meeting with President Obama. "Gun-control advocates will use these provisions to argue that the U.S. must enact measures such as a national gun registry, licenses for guns and ammunition sales, universal background checks, and even a ban of certain weapons. The treaty thus provides the Obama administration with an end-run around Congress to reach these gun-control holy grails."[71]

Nothing in the treaty recognizes civilian ownership of firearms for self-defense or community defense. While the Executive branch already approved and signed the treaty, two-thirds of the Senate must give their advice and consent for ratification. (Art. II, Sec. 2, U.S. Constitution) Then it becomes the "Supreme Law of the Land" under the Constitution's Supremacy Clause.[72]

The Senate voted on a resolution to uphold the Second Amendment and reject the U.N. Arms Trade Treaty on March 3, 2013. The vote was 53 in favor (against the treaty) and 46 opposed (for the treaty).[73]

No Right to Self-Defense

A world-wide umbrella network promoting gun control, the "International Action Network on Small Arms" (IANSA) opposes the use of firearms for self-defense. It advocates prohibiting the private possession of semi-automatic rifles and pistols; it also advocates licensing for any firearms that remain legal.[74] The IANSA represents over 800 gun control organizations in over 100 countries including the United States. Its membership includes America's Brady Campaign, Legal Community Against Violence and the Coalition to Stop Gun Violence (the umbrella network of U.S. organizations).

IANSA, along with Amnesty International and Oxfam International, run the "Control Arms" campaign. Goals include implementation of the Arms Trade Treaty and a global tracking system for all small arms.

IANSA member Barbara Frey, a professor at the University of Michigan and Director of its Human Rights Program, wrote a report on small arms for the U.N. Human Rights Council. The Council appointed her as a Special Rapporteur to study the prevention of human rights violations with small arms.

The report delineates "...two legal principles: States' responsibilities under the due diligence standard to take affirmative steps to prevent small arms abuses by non-State actors and the implications of the principle of self-defense upon the State's small arms policies."[75] The term "State," in this context, means country or nation.

Mrs. Frey's report says that: "Under the due diligence standard, international human rights bodies should require States to enforce a minimum licensing standard designed to prevent small arms from being used by private actors to violate human rights."[76] She does not endorse self-defense as a sufficient basis for civilians to possess small arms. "There is no independent or supervening right in international human rights law of self-defense that would require States to provide civilians with access to small arms."[77]

The report also recommends that international bodies require States to implement two of the most controversial concepts in America's gun debate. We call them assault weapon bans and universal background checks. Frey uses "prohibition of civilian possession of...semi-automatic assault rifles" and the "requirement of...tracing information" to describe those ideas in her report.[78]

The European Union (EU) has directed that its members have all firearms registered by December 2014 and for only holders of government licenses to own guns.[79] Official authorization to own a firearm will require "good cause shown," which does not include self-defense.[80] Quoting Anne-Marie Slaughter, an Obama administration State Department official, the *Wall Street Journal* said: "American transnationalists look with admiration on Europe. 'Once those laws are passed, EU institutions...look over national shoulders to ensure that they actually do what they commit to do,' Ms. Slaughter has written, 'This European way of law is precisely the role that we postulate for International law generally around the world'."[81]

Domestic Change

The broader argument mentioned in O'Brien's Messaging Guide includes disagreement over the meaning of the Second Amendment, the value of gun control to stop or reduce violence and the appropriateness of self-defense. Both sides of these issues express certitude that they have the correct position. According to Pia Carusone, Executive Director of former Congresswoman Gabrielle Gifford's group, Americans for Responsible Solutions, "There is a collective sense that we are on the right side of history" after a meeting of gun control advocates and Joe Biden.[82]

As of this writing, a guaranteed "gun fight" looms ahead with the 2014 Congressional elections. Referring to a vote on gun control by Connecticut legislators in February 2013, Vice President Biden threatened, "If you are concerned about your political survival, you should be concerned about the survival of our children. And guess what? I say there will be a political price to pay for those who refuse to act."[83]

According to the *Wall Street Journal*: "President Obama's vast gun-control agenda, unveiled in January, was never designed to pass this Congress. Its purpose was to rile up Americans and inflict political pain on the party that stood in the way."[84] Obama, referring to the 2014 elections and the 2013 gun-control bill, said: "If this Congress refuses to listen to the American people and pass common-sense gun legislation, then the real impact is going to have to come from the voters."[85] He went on to urge listeners to let their representatives know that "you will remember come election time" and tell them "you have to send the right people to Washington."[86]

New York Mayor Michael Bloomberg said of the Senate vote: "The only silver lining is that we now know who refuses to stand with the 90% of Americans – and in 2014, our ever-expanding coalition of supporters will work to make sure that voters don't forget."[87] "The New York billionaire threw $2.3 million into an Illinois special primary [in March], to help a gun-control Democrat defeat a gun-rights Democrat.

His super PAC is boasting the race will be its model for future elections."[88]

"Shortly after the vote, the Progressive Change Campaign Committee announced it would launch an ad campaign targeting Democratic Senators who voted against the bill. Those included Mark Pryor, D-Ark., Mark Begich, D-Alaska, Max Baucus, D-Mont., and Heidi Heitkamp, D-N.D."[89] It appears that gun control advocates will try to make the next election a national referendum on the use of stricter laws – especially background checks – to attempt violence prevention.

Both Bloomberg's organization and Gifford's group contributed to anti-gun Democrat Terry McAuliffe in his campaign to become Virginia's Governor in November 2013. McAuliffe narrowly defeated the pro-gun Republican, Ken Cuccinelli. The national anti-gun resources poured into the campaign probably helped McAuliffe win.

The same organizations and others will support anti-gun candidates in the November 2014 election. Bloomberg's Mayors Against Illegal Guns and the group Moms Demand Action for Gun Sense began the "Everytown for Gun Safety" campaign in April 2014. The effort will ask women to vote based on gun violence prevention stances of candidates, using emotional appeals to mothers to "educate" them.[90]

Giffords' Americans for Responsible Solutions (ARS) has raised many millions of dollars to influence the 2014 election. The campaign, called "Enough," seeks to have universal background checks enacted, as well as stricter gun trafficking legislation. Mayor Bloomberg's organization and the Brady Campaign both assist ARS with the Enough program.[91]

Pro-gun organizations, like the NRA, the National Association for Gun Rights, the National Shooting Sports Foundation, Gun Owners of America and many others will support the other side in each election with similar resources and equal fervor.

Changing the Second Amendment

The "change" pushed so adamantly by the President includes changing the meaning of the Second Amendment. Its fundamental purpose, citizens defending communities against invaders or the lawless, never appears in the words of Barack Obama. "Like most Americans, I believe the Second Amendment guarantees an individual right to bear arms. I respect our strong tradition of gun ownership and the rights of hunters and sportsmen. There are millions of responsible, law-abiding gun owners in America who cherish their right to bear arms for hunting or sport or protection or collection."[92] When he says "protection," he apparently means self-defense in the home.

The President, a Constitutional scholar, says that the Second Amendment covers hunting, shooting sports, collection and home defense. He appears to deny that the arms citizens have the right to keep and bear means those suitable for militia use. This denial ignores both history and the U.S. Supreme Court precedents in *Miller* and *Heller*. Anti-gun forces must deny the militia use aspect of the Constitution in order for their arguments in favor of banning weapons of war to succeed. One argument, made by Michael Waldman, former Clinton speech writer and president of the Brennan Center for Justice at the NYU School of Law, states that "...state militias eventually dissolved."[93] Another argument, made by a number of people and organizations, claims that the National Guard functions as our militia. This means, according to their theory, that no one needs to bear arms, because the Federal government provides weapons for the National Guard. We will address the logic behind these claims, both of which are wrong, in Chapter 7 on Militia.

The next chapter describes and explains the near total lack of compromise in the gun debate. It also discusses the reasons this deadlock and the efforts to break it have caused a national crisis over the issues.

Chapter 4

NO MIDDLE GROUND

Zero Tolerance of the Gun Debate Explained

The Situation

My pro-gun friends insist upon keeping firearms for defense of themselves, their families and their communities. My anti-gun friends do not want citizens to have guns, because some people misuse them to wound or kill innocents. Neither group seems to accept that the other might have valid points.

The anti-gun folks believe only government should have guns, and for some of them, total civilian disarmament is the ultimate goal. "The most extreme gun control zealots will do anything to eliminate guns in America."[1] While not all gun control advocates take this extreme position, many people who own guns and want to keep them see every gun control proposal as a step toward mass domestic disarmament, in great part due to the rhetoric of these "extreme gun control zealots." Advocates for more gun control include most of the media, the current administration, some judges, much of the Democratic Party, and many anti-gun organizations.

The pro-gun side of the debate includes many of the over 100 million gun owners, and there are up to 300 million firearms in approximately half of American homes. Citizens purchased close to a million guns each month in 2013, setting record sales numbers, and the increased demand for both guns and ammunition continues unabated. Nearly every weekend, gun owners attend gun shows where they buy and sell guns, talk about firearms, and discuss politics. Many thousands of people go to each of over 3,000 gun shows every year.[2]

These citizens have the Constitution, history, and Supreme Court precedent in their favor, as well as a number of well-funded, long-standing organizations.

Guns will not disappear, regardless of whatever gun control laws may pass. Guns made in the 19th century still function flawlessly today. "This, by the way, is one of the problems with gun bans; unless we're willing to go house to house rounding them up, the country's 300 million privately owned guns are going to last forever."[3]

Even a house to house search will not work. Millions of Americans will hide their firearms before allowing the government to confiscate them. They will do so in the belief, probably correct, that the Second Amendment justifies their continued possession, regardless of any law to the contrary. "Guns are permanent in America."[4]

The organizations on both sides spend millions of dollars annually, and expend untold thousands of hours in human effort. These groups solicit funds endlessly, playing on the fears of their constituents and milking them to raise money.

This may help explain why an issue Americans generally see as relatively unimportant persists in the media and in our political discourse. Few Americans mention guns as one of the most important problems facing the nation today, despite the attention lawmakers give to the gun debate.[5] Only four percent of respondents think guns and gun control are an important problem facing the country as of April, 2013.[6] Employees of organizations leading the fight on both sides make their living from the gun control debate, and many lawmakers receive major contributions from sources on both sides. Therefore, for the major players, there is far greater financial incentive to prolong the dispute than there is to resolve the issues.

Considering the Middle Ground

Lawmakers and advocates, on both sides, could better serve the people of the United States by resolving the gun debate and putting it behind us. However, we cannot expect a resolution in today's America for two primary reasons, beyond the financial incentive noted above.

First, the anti-gun groups clearly include a substantial number of people who will not rest until America's civilians can no longer legally possess firearms. These "gun grabbers" hope for incremental progress - "baby steps" - from background checks to assault weapons bans, then gun registration, and eventually buy-backs, turn-ins, or outright confiscation.

The second reason Americans cannot reach compromise relates to the first. Pro-gun advocates and so-called "gun nuts" recognize and reject some anti-gun activists' goal of complete citizen disarmament, with many considering the effort treasonous.

Settling the gun control debate would have great value. First, the expenditure of massive resources on the debate would stop. Second, the friction this fight causes between Americans all over the country would end. Third, resolution would provide closure, which should allow the country to move on to other important issues, and would reduce the legal uncertainties about firearms ownership we currently experience. We might even become a little safer.

However, neither side seems to understand that they cannot win this debate. The passions aroused in the aftermath of Sandy Hook saw mixed results. Some states increased restrictions on semi-automatic firearms and their magazines, while others eased laws on concealed carry, self-defense, and ownership. The President's all out push for gun control "change" failed in the Senate, in part, because *Democrats* voted against it.

Everyone stands ready to renew the fight. Each subsequent high profile shooting event will see anti-gun professionals and "spokespersons" re-energized in an effort to take advantage of media attention and exploit the sympathy we all feel for the victims. The pro-gun advocates will renew their push for reciprocal concealed carry and registration prohibitions and similar initiatives. Sales of firearms and ammunition will skyrocket again. Money, time, and effort will be expended on both sides, to little avail. The pressures for disarmament will continue to clash with the need for self- defense, and the pushback from both sides will only grow more intense and confrontational.

Finality Is Needed, Not "Progress"

If representatives of each side could meet to discuss settlement and honestly believed in resolving this conflict, the next step would challenge all concerned. They would have to agree that the resulting full and final settlement has permanence, and that no one could later try to enact more laws in their favor. In other words, the incremental or "progressive" efforts to implement gun control, as well as the similar effort to expand gun rights, would have to stop.

Since no mechanism to enforce finality exists, actual settlement of most gun issues cannot take place. Gun rights defenders realize that their opponents use the "one-step-at-a-time" technique. This causes them to be adamant in their opposition to all proposals for compromise. The method goes by a number of names, such as "camel's-nose-under-the-tent, foot-in-the-door," or "slippery slope." President Obama has, on several occasions, alluded to following such a course.

Addressing the nation after his second inauguration, the President said: "Progress does not compel U.S. to settle centuries-long debates about the role of government for all time but it does require U.S. to act in our time."[7] He refers to the Virginia Tech and Newtown shootings, then goes on to say: "We must act knowing that our work will be imperfect. We must act, knowing that today's victories will be only partial and that it will be up to those who stand here in four years and 40 years and 400 years hence to advance..."[8]

President Obama talks about progress again in his speech on gun control at the Denver Police Academy: "We're not going to just wait for the next Newtown or the next Aurora before we act. And I genuinely believe that's what the overwhelming majority of Americans – I don't care what party they belong to – that's what they want. They just want to see some progress."[9]

President Obama spoke about progress yet again in the context of the failed Senate gun control bill and its background check amendment. "So while this compromise didn't contain everything I wanted or everything that these [Sandy Hook] families wanted, it did represent progress."[10] In this context, progress means: proceeding in steps; continuing steadily by increments; progressive change proceeding by degrees; moving successfully from one stage to the next, gradually advancing in extent; ever widening scope. It follows the strategy of accumulation.

The concept of accumulation involves making small changes when and where possible to eventually accomplish huge results. These minor moves, over time, accumulate to eventually produce the desired major change.[11]

When gun control advocates succeed on an issue, they use the accumulation approach and shift their focus to another issue, using the momentum of their most recent success to continue moving steadily toward their ultimate objective: Gun laws in the United States similar to those passed in Australia and the United Kingdom. In other words, the disarming of all civilians. Pro-gun activists have adopted the same approach and countered in kind, expanding rights wherever and whenever possible. Each side knows how the other's strategy works, so no one will compromise.

The Issues

One side of the debate over guns thinks that the U.S. needs to eventually disarm all people. The other side wants "the people" to permanently keep and, if necessary, have the ability to use firearms for defense of family, community, and country. Neither side believes that violent criminals or the dangerously insane should have weapons. Unfortunately, this area of agreement has little or no relationship to the issues.

Background Checks

Why did the Senate background check amendment fail in April, 2013? First, the 60-vote requirement procedure chosen by the President and Majority Leader Reid kept it from passing by a simple majority. They opted to maintain the 60-vote rule in order to prevent other, pro-gun amendments from passing, and to prevent full debate. Second, the universal aspect, which would force formal background checks even for transfers between family, friends and neighbors, offended many gun owners. Third, the aforementioned progressive, one-step-at-a-time approach to gun restrictions ensured resistance to any encroachment on rights. Many Americans saw this amendment as the next step in the progress toward registration and confiscation.

The data the government would collect during universal checks appeared to provide a future administration with tools to assist with confiscation, should the incremental efforts for total civilian disarmament ever succeed. The details of each transaction would eventually find their way into Federal computers, and many simply do not trust that the information would not be misused.

The Obama Administration wants universal background checks to bring America in compliance with the U.N. Small Arms Treaty, also known as the Arms Trade Treaty (A.T.T.). The U.S. voted for a U.N.

resolution in favor of the treaty on April 2, 2013. Secretary of State John Kerry signed it after meeting with President Obama at the U.N. in New York, making the U.S. an official signatory on September 25, 2013. Two-thirds of the Senate must ratify the treaty for it to become "the law of the land," but the President seems committed to implementing it now, despite the fact that a clear majority of Senators oppose the treaty.[12] This explains the pivot after high profile shooting events, from horror and sympathy to the call for universal background checks. Background checks for *all* transfers meets the U.N. treaty's tracing requirements. The treaty calls for governments to develop the ability to trace all firearms from manufacturers to end users, including target rifles and pistols, hunting guns, and collectibles.

A number of sources report that universal background checks will have very little impact on the number of guns used in crime.[13] As noted in a previous chapter, nearly all of the guns used in recent high-profile shootings would still have found their way to the shooter's hands if a universal background check law had applied. The shootings at Virginia Tech; Aurora, Colorado; Fort Hood; the Navy Yard, and many others involved guns legally acquired with a background check. In other cases, like Columbine and Sandy Hook, crimes had been committed in the way the shooters acquired their guns, for example, illegal straw purchases (Columbine), and theft (Sandy Hook – after having murdered the legal owner). Since not one major shooting would have been prevented by universal background checks, the only logical explanation for the focus of the administration on expanded checks appears to be the desire to meet the U.N. tracing requirements.

Abramski v. U.S.

A criminal case about background checks and straw purchases was argued before the U.S. Supreme Court on January 22, 2014. The case originated in the Western District of Virginia, one of the courts in which I practice.

Mr. Abramski answered "yes" to the question: "Are you the actual transferee/buyer of the firearm listed on the form?" Upon receipt of the firearm, a Glock 19, he shipped it to a licensed dealer in Pennsylvania, who then transferred it to Abramski's uncle, who had provided the funds for purchase.

Charged as an illegal "straw purchaser," Abramski argued that since both he and his uncle were legally entitled to purchase the Glock, no crime had occurred.[14]

During oral argument before the Supreme Court, Joseph R. Palmore argued for the United States that "...the one critical purpose of the (background check) statute, obviously was to keep firearms out of the hands of ineligible persons, but another critical purpose was to offer the tracing of firearms and to prevent the anonymous stockpiling of firearms."[15] Palmore went on to explain that the lack of accurate tracing information recorded at the point of sale background check "...would greatly impair the ability of the ATF to trace firearms."[16] The Court agreed with the government, upholding the Abramski conviction in a five to four vote (*Abramski v U.S.*, 573 U.S.___(2014), Doc #12-1493).

Gun Shows and Background Checks

Gun shows draw millions of attendees every year. Sales by dealers – with background checks – often happen almost instantly at most shows. Many other sales, by individuals who carry a gun or two to the show, or by exhibitors of small, private collections, occur without background checks.

I began working at gun shows when a friend of my father asked for my help in the early 1970s. He needed someone to assist with set-up, to watch the table when he left it to look at displays on other tables or to use the restroom, as well as to help with taking down his display when the show ended. Although I was a young teenager at the time, this experience later helped me land a paying job helping a dealer with shows. I worked several shows every year, until I graduated from high school and left for college.

Many years later, after college, military duty, and law school, I returned to gun shows as a social and business sideline. I soon decided to become a Federally licensed firearms dealer (FFL) and expanded my gun show activities.

About ten years ago I developed an interest in acting as a dealer for law enforcement agencies, including fully automatic machine guns in my offerings. I added a "Class 3" or Special Occupation Tax stamp (SOT) to my FFL, which authorized me to buy and sell machineguns. After a year or so, I switched my focus from selling law enforcement guns to participating in the national Class 3 market, dealing in collectible, transferable machine guns.

Learning about and dealing in the collectible machine gun market took me to gun shows all around the country. In addition to shows in my home state of Virginia, I manned tables as a dealer in Arizona, Kentucky, Nevada, and Pennsylvania. I also attended shows in the Carolinas, Maryland, Oklahoma, and several other states.

All dealers at gun shows realize that transactions - both sales and trades - occur constantly between private parties without "paper" or a background check. The aisles, stairwells, parking lots and sidewalks provide venues to make a purchase or trade without government involvement. Exhibitors with private collections and show attendees can legitimately sell without checks under Federal law. However, some states, such as California and Colorado, require all transfers to include a background check.

When someone not legally qualified to possess a firearm buys a gun, he or she commits a crime. The seller also commits a crime, if he knows that the purchaser does not qualify. Background checks attempt to prevent unqualified transactions by an administrative procedure. Historically, very few failed background checks have resulted in prosecution of the prospective purchaser, who had apparently committed perjury on the background check form.

If the checks stop illegal transfers, even though they have no effect on the use of guns in crime, why do gun-owners and dealers object? It would seem that dealers should want everyone to have to perform the same checks they must, if for no other reason, to level the playing field with the competition. From my experience observing many thousands of people at over a hundred gun shows, I know of three basic reasons that the firearms community does not want universal background checks.

First, buyers do not like the extra expense incurred when purchasing from a dealer. The transfer fee is minimal ($2.00 in Virginia), but they really hate paying sales tax (6% in Virginia).

Second, background checks can take unacceptable amounts of time. The buyer has to spend time filling out forms and the seller takes time to call in or electronically submit the request to the NICS system. The response can take from as little as a few seconds to as long as several days. Since gun shows normally last two days and close by 4 P.M. to 5 P.M. each day, a slow response time can cause lost sales. Vendors and their customers often come from distant locations and cannot close a deal with a delayed response.

The third, and by far the most important reason for objections to background checks, revolves around the belief that government has no business tracking the sale of firearms. Otherwise upstanding, law abiding citizens want no part of creating a computer record of their gun purchases. They fear that those records will later provide information to authorities who will demand buy-backs, turn-ins, or registration. Once registration occurs, confiscation seems a likely next step in the effort to either subjugate people or, at a minimum, prevent them from having an effective means of self-defense. The active gun suppression units in California and Illinois give credence to these concerns.

This helps explain why the Senate's 2013 Gun Control Bill and its Background Check Amendment failed. The concern about computer records of gun ownership, combined with the perceived need to deny anti-gun forces' progress, prevents the willingness to compromise on any measure that would result in universal background checks.

Assault Weapons

After Universal Background Checks, anti-gun groups' next major goal is to enact a new Federal ban on assault weapons. Many Americans resist this ban because they see the civilian versions of modern service rifles and pistols as the best firearms for "militia purposes" and self-defense. Here too, neither side wants to compromise.

Ban advocates know that the use of guns that meet the assault weapon definition in high profile crimes makes their argument a strong one. A Federal ban on semi-automatic rifles would also move the United States closer to the apparent U.N. goal of reducing the power of civilians. Crime prevention appears to have little or nothing to do with the actual reasoning behind the bans.

The National Institute of Justice says that "assault weapons are not a major contributor to gun crime." It goes on to advise that "an assault weapon ban is unlikely to have an impact on gun violence." The study also suggests that "a complete elimination of assault weapons would not have a large impact on gun homicides."[17]

Opponents see a ban as both another step in the progress toward complete civilian disarmament and a clear violation of the Second Amendment. Again, neither side indicates that there is any middle ground on this issue.

Magazine Capacity

The idea of banning magazines which hold more than a certain number of cartridges relates closely to that of banning so-called assault weapons. In theory, this would limit or reduce the number of shots a wrongdoer could fire and, therefore, lower the amount of damage done. Magazine bans would also serve as another step on the path to eliminating the guns themselves.

Several states have banned "ammunition feeding devices" - detachable magazines - with capacities greater than a set number of rounds. Colorado allows no more than 15 rounds, while New York passed an 8 round limit. A number of states, including Connecticut, have outlawed magazines holding over 10 cartridges.

Many experts find these bans somewhat silly, as well as unconstitutional. The silliness comes, at least in part, from the ease with which shooters can avoid the purpose of magazine bans. Anyone with the slightest training and practice can change magazines in a second or two. The changes do not require an empty chamber, so guns need not ever run "dry" or empty. Carrying two or more handguns will also defeat the reason for the bans. Furthermore, the huge number of magazines with higher capacities already in civilian hands - estimates range as high as *several hundred million* - precludes the effectiveness of such bans.

The U.S. Supreme Court could, and if it follows its precedent, should, find the state bans and any future Federal ban on some magazines unconstitutional. Certainly the M1A service rifle 20 round magazine, the M16/AR-15 service rifle 20 and 30 round versions and the Beretta M9/92F service pistol's 15 round magazine all comprise "...part of the ordinary military equipment" the use of which "...could contribute to the common defense," as contemplated in *Miller*.[18] They also fit the definition of military items "...in common use" today.[19]

The *Heller* Court reiterated this idea in its discussion of *Miller*.[20]

Regardless of how the courts rule, removing magazines from civilian ownership would prove to be practically impossible. They do not have serial numbers, their size makes them easy to hide, the sheer number involved staggers imagination, and most importantly, many Americans would not cooperate with the bans.

Connecticut's ban on high capacity magazines allowed the "grandfathering" of those already in the hands of citizens, as long as owners registered the magazines with the State Police by December 31, 2013. People registered approximately 40,000 of the estimated *one to two million* affected magazines. Whether intentionally or not, many thousands of Connecticut's citizens have now violated their state's criminal laws.

Gun owners might be willing to compromise on bans of aftermarket 50 to 100 round drum magazines or extra capacity, extended pistol magazines in return for leaving standard service rifle and pistol versions alone, were it not for the "progressive" aspect of the bans. The problem of the "one-step-at-a-time" approach joins the other reasons for opposing a ban on magazines. The high-capacity magazine ban, like an assault weapons ban, seems another issue destined for continued disagreement and eventual resolution in the Supreme Court.

Concealed Carry

The issuance of concealed carry permits has become another issue headed for the U.S. Supreme Court. Reciprocity, or the requirement to honor the permits issued by other states, also remains a contentious question, as does the use of deadly force in self-defense, especially outside the home.

On one extreme, some states allow the carrying of concealed weapons in public without any permit. Others, on the opposite extreme, have very strict requirements for training and demonstration of "need" before issuing a permit. Most have laws that fall somewhere between the extremes, and all states now have some provision for legal concealed carry.

A three judge panel of the U.S. 9th Circuit Court of Appeals recently overturned a San Diego County, California requirement for applicants desiring a concealed carry permit to demonstrate "need" to carry concealed. Called a "good cause regime," the rules did not allow simple self-defense as sufficient cause to grant a concealed carry permit application.[21] The 7th Circuit agrees with the 9th, while the 2nd, 3rd and 4th Circuits ruled the other way. State Supreme Courts have also split on this issue.

The *Heller* case made it clear that people have the right to keep a handgun at home for defense, but did not address the question of carrying firearms in public for self-defense. The coming full panel review by the 9th Circuit may change the three-judge panel ruling in *Peruta*, but the Supreme Court will almost certainly have to resolve the split at some point in the future.

Both the people who believe only law enforcement should carry guns and those who want citizens to have concealed carry rights seem resolute in their beliefs. We can add concealed carry to the irreconcilable difference list, where middle ground is hard to find.

Straw Purchases

A "straw purchase" occurs when someone buys a gun on behalf of another person who cannot legally possess a firearm. The buyer typically passes a background check and pays the licensed dealer. He or she then gives the gun to the real purchaser, who could not have passed the background check. The prohibited person usually bribes or has some leverage over the straw purchaser. This type of purchase requires perjury by the fake buyer on the ATF transfer form required for dealer sales, because the form requires the buyer to answer under oath whether he or she is the actual purchaser.

Since the frequency of such transfers surpasses theft as a source of firearms used by criminals, most people can agree that focusing law enforcement effort on illegal sales to prohibited persons makes sense. According to the National Institute of Justice: "Straw purchasers are the primary source of crime guns."[22]

"Because straw purchasers are the largest source for the illicit market, and these purchasers likely can be deterred, effort should be focused here."[23] The solution to stopping straw purchases is another area where agreement is lacking. Law enforcement officials have difficulty detecting when the buyer uses someone else's money to buy a gun. The nature of the transaction eliminates the effectiveness of background checks, because the actual purchaser picks a person who can pass the background check to make the buy.

Doctor Ridgeway recommends that *all* firearms transfers require a background check by an FFL. This would mean accepting universal background checks. He then explains that the effectiveness of these checks to reduce crime will also require gun registration, saying that: "Universal checks are insufficient for ensuring that firearms owners remain eligible."[24] Registration poses serious practical and Constitutional problems so once again, Americans lack middle ground for settling the issue.

Registration

Registration clearly infringes upon the right to bear arms under the Supreme Court cases to date. It is also plagued with huge practical problems, even if future lawmakers and Courts decide that the government has the "need to know" who owns what guns. The current firearms registry, begun in the 1930s under the National Firearms Act (NFA) for machine guns, silencers, short barreled rifles and shotguns, destructive devices, and other weapons, demonstrates the inability of the U.S. government to manage registration efficiently.

Transfers of machine guns from licensed dealers to legally qualified purchasers currently take up to 15 months or more for ATF approval. Each transfer results in an ATF agent (examiner) reviewing the transfer form (ATF Form 4 for private citizens), issuing an approval and changing the registration from the seller to the buyer. Even transfers between licensed dealers (ATF Form 3) often take several months.

Transfer response times for the existing registry show that broader registration will defy the government's ability to manage the effort. Imagine the results if an agency that takes over a year to process a few thousand annual transactions tries to handle millions per year. Add a change from a registry tracking a few million items at most to one tracking over 300 million items. This hundredfold increase simply would not work.

The other reason registration will not work involves civil disobedience. Literally millions of firearms would not make the registry and millions of Americans would break the law. Millions, if not tens of millions of people believe that registration violates the Constitution and that they should not obey an unconstitutional law.

A future, activist Supreme Court could reinterpret the Second Amendment to allow national registration, but millions will hide at least some of their guns rather than comply. Despite a number of amnesty periods to allow more registration, this has already happened with an unknown number of machine guns. Anecdotal stories abound of World War II veterans' "bring back" of unregistered guns, hidden in closets, attics, under floors, and otherwise tucked away.

The state of Connecticut passed a new, stricter assault weapons ban in April, 2013. The law allowed civilians to keep firearms defined as assault weapons, as long as they registered the guns with the State Police by December 31, 2013. Estimates of the number of firearms affected range from 150,000 to 350,000. The State Police had received approximately 50,000 applications for registration by the deadline. The new law has, in effect, turned large numbers of otherwise law-abiding Connecticut citizens into felons.

The Constitutional problems, impracticality, and unenforceability make registration a concept without room for compromise. The firearms community sees it as the last step before confiscation, and will never agree or, if Connecticut is an example, comply with a law that requires registering commonly owned guns.

Secure Storage

The opposite applies to secure storage. Americans should readily agree that encouraging firearms security merits attention. "An estimated half-million guns a year go missing in the U.S. and end up in criminal hands."[25] Gun safes, alarm systems and other techniques could drastically reduce this problem. As Dan Baum correctly points out, if people learned and used proper storage "the problem with unsecured guns – the main source of gun tragedy – would wither away."[26]

The government could help by giving tax credits for purchasing gun safes and for the cost of secure storage classes. We should include secure storage training in hunter education, concealed carry courses, and anywhere else it would be appropriate. We could also consider incentives for alarm systems. Talk about real "common sense" measures! Preventing physical access to other people's guns by criminals, children, and the mentally ill should come first among ideas to solve "gun violence." Perhaps middle ground can be found and compromise will work for this issue.

Self-Defense

Self-defense rules could stand uniformity and on the surface, would seem to be another area where compromise should be possible. Pro-gun groups like "Stand-Your-Ground" laws and the "Castle Doctrine." Both of these concepts allow people to legally use lethal force in response to threats of severe harm or death. Stand-Your-Ground laws apply in public, while the Castle Doctrine treats a person's home as his or her "castle." Both concepts allow the use of force *without* an attempt to avoid conflict. Anti-gun violence forces call them "shoot first" or "kill at will" laws.

A reasonable settlement of this issue could result from eliminating one and embracing the other. When in public, running, hiding, screaming or otherwise making deadly force a last resort makes sense. An armed citizen could still use their weapon if all else fails, but not if unnecessary. So why not a national trade of Stand-Your-Ground for the Castle Doctrine?

Allowing force in response to a threat of violence inside one's home seems perfectly reasonable. Under the Castle Doctrine, no retreat or other avoidance tactic has to be attempted before responding to a home invasion or other deadly threat with lethal weapons.

Since the advocates at the extremes of the gun debate seem to want compromise only as progress toward larger goals, even fairly reasonable middle ground proposals on self-defense such as these will probably fail.

School Security

Real common sense should prevail in providing school security. Declaring schools "gun free" and locking the doors did not and will not stop a determined shooter. Newtown showed us all that a sick, violent person can easily ignore laws and overcome passive security measures. Sandy Hook Elementary School had state of the art modern physical security, and Connecticut has some of the nation's strongest gun control laws, all to no avail.

The people who worry about the "message" children will receive if armed people guard them either miss the point or lack a grasp of reality. Only a person with the capacity to stop an Adam Lanza on site, at that moment, can prevent someone like him from killing children. We need to send the message that we will not allow our children to suffer physical harm.

I can remember no greater comfort as a child than knowing the people around me, mostly relatives, would not allow anyone to harm children. Mostly law enforcement officers, former military, and their family members, my parents, uncles, cousins, neighbors and their friends kept rifles, pistols and shotguns near to hand, just in case. They knew that "sick" criminals existed in the world and stayed vigilant to make sure we all lived safely. My father called these dangerous criminals the "one percent." He thought that approximately one person out of a hundred would hurt or kill others if allowed to act freely.

This tradition of armed vigilance came from centuries of history, and the message we learned as children had two aspects. First, we felt treasured and safe. Second, as we grew older, we knew our turn as protectors would come.

The world has not changed so much that we can realistically count on laws and locks to stop insanity or violence. We should have resource officers, trained school staff, trained parent volunteers, or whatever it takes to assure that an attacker will not succeed. This particular issue may not need addressing as part of the gun control debate, but because school shooting events result in calls for more laws, it warrants discussion. If we cannot find middle ground on any other subject, this one deserves a real, practical solution, for the sake of our children's safety.

Safety

The resources expended on the political debate over guns and gun control seem terribly wasted. A focus on safety training and education would far better serve Americans than the divisive clash over gun control laws. While organizations on both sides of the divide have good ideas about teaching safety, the two sides show little promise of working together towards actually making people safer.

Conclusion

Middle ground on gun issues does not seem to exist, although it should for secure storage and school security, at a minimum. Professional advocates on both sides have too much to gain from fanning the flames of emotions to want a final compromise. Many citizens think that no civilians should have arms and simply want to see progress toward the elimination of guns in America. People who believe in the rights of citizens to defend themselves and their communities with firearms also believe they cannot maintain those rights if they give in to compromise and allow that progress.

However, the anti-gun movement continues to grow, in both numbers and financial resources. This growth, combined with international efforts and a member of the movement in the White House, puts serious negative pressure on the Second Amendment. This pressure has resulted in progress against the right to keep and bear arms in several state legislatures and courts. The movement also plans to unleash a major anti-gun political campaign in advance of the 2014 and 2016 elections, as described in Chapter 3, with no middle ground in sight.

The next chapter summarizes the history of America's Second Amendment arms. Hopefully, along with the chapter on militia, it will help provide perspective for understanding how the Second Amendment applies in the 21st century.

Chapter 5

WEAPONS FOR WAR:

Firearms in Battles From Jamestown To The 21st Century

When the first Englishmen came to America, they carried three types of hand-held firearms: Matchlocks, wheellocks, and snaphaunces. The initial landing party of the Jamestown settlement went ashore at Cape Henry on the Chesapeake Bay in April, 1607. The party was immediately attacked by Indians and driven back to the ship.

On May 14 of that year they went ashore again to establish the colony called Jamestown. From the moment they set foot on the New World, the colonists lived in constant fear of attack. Historian D.A. Tisdale wrote, "The island was chosen because of its ease of defense against the Indians, and against any Spanish who might appear."[1] About two weeks after the Colonists' arrival, native bowmen attacked them again, but after an hour long battle, their musket fire and ship's cannon repelled the attack.

Following several minor conflicts with Indians, the colony faced sporadic sieges by the natives. These attacks intensified between November of 1609 through May of 1610, by which point only 90 colonists had survived. Fortunately for the remaining colonists, on May 24th, another 135 men arrived, followed by 100 more in June. Many of these 235 men were veterans of military service in Europe. They had brought their personal weapons as well as some provided by the Crown, the majority of which, as noted previously, were matchlocks, wheellocks, and snaphaunces.[2]

The wheellock uses an ignition system not unlike an old-fashioned cigarette lighter. When the wheel spins, it generates a spark that ignites a small charge of priming powder, which in turn causes the main powder charge to explode, sending the bullet down the barrel. A shooter "cocks" the wheel by tightening a spring with a key or wrench, much like winding a mechanical clock.

The matchlock has a burning wick (the "match") attached to a "cock" (named for its resemblance to the head and beak of a cock rooster) which holds the match above the priming powder. Upon pulling the trigger, the match drops into the priming powder, which ignites the primary charge through the flash hole, causing the gun to fire.

Snaphaunces used a piece of flint to create spark. The "cock" was the mechanism that the shooter pulled back, against spring tension, and which fell forward suddenly when the trigger was pulled, causing the flint to strike a metal plate and create an igniting spark.

Dampness reduced the effectiveness of the matchlock and snaphaunce, and the user found them, along with the wheellock, cumbersome to reload. All three types had a significant delay between the pulling of the trigger and the discharge of the lead ball, known as "lock time," which required some skill to manage for any sort of accuracy. None of these firearms fired accurately at ranges past a few dozen yards, with the exception of some wheellocks. Rifling had been invented and, while difficult to manufacture, German, Austrian, and Italian gunmakers installed rifled barrels on some of the more expensive wheellock arms used in the late 1500s and early 1600s.

Experience with spinning arrows and crossbow bolts had taught gunmakers that imparting a spin to a projectile offered an obvious benefit, by increasing accuracy and useful range. Their experiments with early rifling proved that the same benefit could be realized by causing the bullet to spin and therefore stabilize, giving the firearm significantly more accuracy. At the time, however, only the wealthiest colonists could afford these very high-priced wheellock rifles.[3]

Wheellock rifle manufacture continued until the flintlock became the preferred design. "By the early seventeenth century [the flintlock] was more or less standard on all firearms."[4]

The flintlock began to arrive in Virginia by the 1620s, and while many undoubtedly continued to use older forms of firearms, the flintlock gradually became the primary type for defense. "In 1676, of 1500 muskets sent to the colony by Charles II, 1200 were flintlock weapons."[5] The flintlock had a flat piece of steel forged to the flash pan cover so that as soon as the shooter placed priming powder in the pan and lowered the cover he could fire. The flint held in the cock would strike this piece of steel upon its release by the trigger pull. The resulting spark caused the priming powder in the pan to "flash" through a hole into the chamber, igniting the main powder charge. This charge exploded powerfully enough to push a lead ball out of the barrel at speeds of several hundred feet per second.

The term "flash in the pan" comes from a failed flintlock firing attempt where the priming powder flashes in the pan, but fails to ignite the main charge in the chamber. This "misfire" might look like a fired shot, but no bullet is launched, which often resulted in problems, particularly in a defensive situation or on the battlefield.

It was soon discovered that this improved firing mechanism needed a "lock" position to prevent accidental discharge when loading or carrying the gun. With a "half-cock" safety arrangement or locking mechanism, in the half-cock position, the cock with the flint could not fall and strike the pan, and the musket or rifle would not fire, even if the shooter pulled the trigger.

The function of this design was probably the origin of the military command, "lock and load." Some version of this locking mechanism stayed in use by the U.S. military until the 1890s. The last weapon used by American soldiers that required locking before loading was the trap door rifle. With the hammer at half-cock, the door would open and the soldier inserted a cartridge by hand. The door then latched so that the rifle could then be brought to full cock, and ready to fire.

"Early in the 18th century, the last matchlocks were withdrawn from service and the flintlock was in general use by all troops in the British army. What might be called the standard weapon of this type appeared early in the 18th century and, although the name was apparently not recorded until much later in the century, this musket is known to all collectors as the "Brown Bess."[6] The flintlock musket design worked well for massed short-range fire. It could also have a bayonet attached for defense against cavalry or close fighting with enemy troops. However, because of its smooth bore, the musket was practically useless for accurate, aimed fire. The colonists needed something better for both hunting and defense. The flintlock rifle provided an answer to that problem.

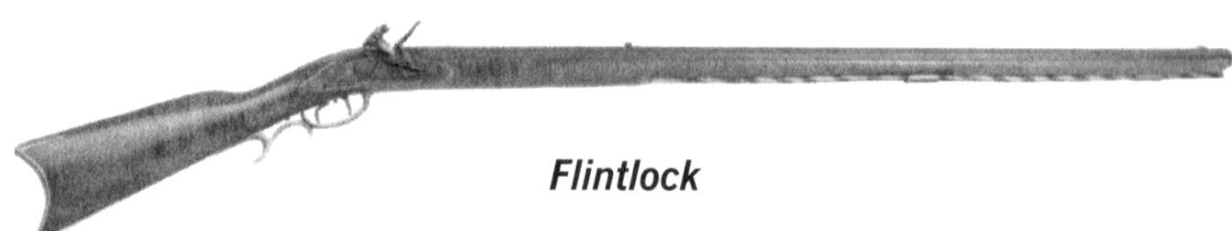

Flintlock

"Among those who immigrated to North America during the 18th century were gunmakers from Europe who were well experienced in rifling barrels. They continued plying their trade in the new country, and gradually evolved a distinctive weapon. Appearing during the early 18th century, this rifle had a long barrel and fired a relatively small lead ball. Known as the Pennsylvania or Kentucky Rifle, it soon acquired a distinctive shape, and by the late 18th century had a characteristic, gracefully down-curving butt frequently decorated with inlaid brass."[7]

Militia used these rifles to fight during the Indian Wars, in the American Revolution, and again in the War of 1812.

These battles demonstrated the superiority of the civilian militia's rifle in some situations, as well as the value of a militia armed with muskets. However, civilian rifles would not take a bayonet and reloaded more slowly than a musket. Rifle design usually included relatively delicate stocks that, unlike military muskets, did not permit their use as a club. Therefore, they did not fare well in close combat with mass formations. In one specific example, once the militia at Bunker Hill's gunpowder ran out, most of the militiamen retreated, leaving the battlefield to the British.

The new country of the United States of America needed firearms in case of further war. The new government contracted with gunmakers for "militia muskets" after declaring the Constitution in March, 1792 and passing the first Militia Act of May, 1792. Gunmakers designed the "Militia Musket" to arm the state militia. The original New England flintlock Militia Musket of 1792 was a dual purpose musket/fowler of .70 caliber. This firearm served both as a hunting shotgun for civilian use and a militia weapon in case of war by combining the features of the civilian hunting guns and military weapons.

The United States produced its first military musket at the Springfield Armory in Massachusetts. Called the Model 1795 Musket or 1795 Springfield, the weapon greatly resembled the French Model 1763 Charleville Musket, from which it was derived.

The new U.S. Army adopted the image of crossed 1795 muskets as the symbol for infantry soldiers., an insignia still used by the Army's Infantry branch today.

Militia Muskets and 1795 Military Muskets saw extensive use in battle from the War of 1812 through the Civil War (often after conversion to percussion). Both had a "club stock" for hand-to-hand fighting. The typical civilian stock extended to the end of the muzzle, but the militia version's forestock stopped a few inches behind the front sight so that a bayonet could be affixed. Individuals and state governments purchased these muskets to increase the number of armed citizens.

The term "fowler" in the late 1700s equates to today's "shotgun." More precisely, the Militia Musket could be used as a muzzle loading version of the modern single-shot shotgun. Settlers used fowlers to hunt game birds or "fowl," such as quail, grouse, pheasants, turkeys, woodcock, snipe, ducks and geese. Firing a large number of small lead pellets (shot), these smoothbore guns produced a pattern or spread of shot which, if properly placed, would drop a flying bird. When loaded with a ball, the fowler became a .70 caliber musket for military use. The Militia musket also cost a good deal less than a rifle to manufacture, so it allowed many more American citizens to afford a firearm suitable for both hunting and defense.

Rifles continued to serve as the preferred firearms for hunting most fur-bearing game, like squirrels and deer. Due to the smaller caliber of most rifles, they used less powder and lead (both expensive) than a fowler, in addition to having longer range and far better accuracy.

Riflemen took great pride in accurate shooting. Each shot on game needed to make a clean kill to conserve ammunition and avoid damaging the meat. Precision shooting required great skill and those who mastered it considered good marksmanship an important accomplishment. These men originated the "one shot, one kill" philosophy of military snipers.[8]

During Texas quest for independence, its militia fought a number of battles with Indians and Mexicans, with individual citizens providing most of their own rifles, rather than the weapons being issued to them by the Texas government. The common firearms of that time remained the flintlock muskets and rifles, although the new "caplock" found its way to some battles.[9]

The caplock used a percussion cap on a hollow metal cylinder called a "nipple" for its priming system. The "hammer" (no longer looking like a "cock," but you still "cocked" it) would crush the cap, which had an explosive priming compound inside a copper sleeve. A spark would then go through the hole in the nipple into the chamber to ignite the powder and discharge the firearm. Percussion technology resulted in far fewer failures to fire due to powder dampness than flintlocks, and the guns were able to be reloaded more quickly. The first American military caplock, the U.S. model 1842 musket, had a smooth bore. "The model 1842 saw continuous production from 1844 until 1855, when it was succeeded by the rifle musket."[10] During this time civilians preferred the caplock rifle, which combined the percussion cap technology with the accuracy of a rifled bore.

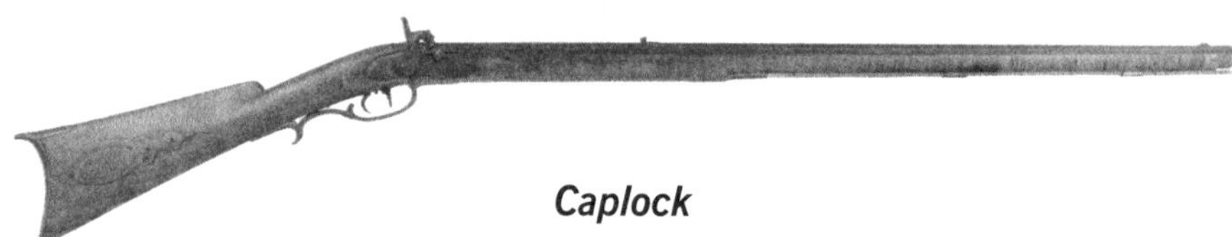

Caplock

Muskets and rifles each have three primary components, the lock, stock, and barrel. The saying "lock, stock and barrel" still means "the whole thing" today. The lock, or ignition system, attached to the rear of the barrel, and the stock held both to make a firearm. Screws, bands or some other form of attachments firmly connected these parts to each other.

Barrels, usually a long piece of steel in a round or octagonal shape, had several features. The "bore," a long hole along the barrel's center, allowed the projectile to travel at high speeds from the end near the ignition source to and out of the "muzzle" into the air. The diameter of a bore had more than one descriptive term, with "caliber" the most common in America, expressed in fractions of inches. Smooth bore guns for firing bullets or solid balls were called muskets or smoothbores. Rifled barrels instead of the smooth bored barrel resulted in the name rifle or rifled musket. The portion of the barrel at the ignition point that holds the gunpowder and ball, or cartridge in modern rifles, acted as the "chamber." Sights affixed to the top of the barrel allowed the shooter to aim at the target.

Weapons commonly used during this period included the U.S. Model 1842 musket, militia muskets converted from flint to percussion, and caplock rifles. The rifled musket using a caplock percussion system became the principal weapon used by both sides in the American Civil War.

American Civil War

Union forces used the 1861 Springfield rifled musket, which was manufactured in the Springfield armory in Massachusetts. Similar rifles, such as the 1861 Special Musket made by Colt's Manufacturing Company located in Hartford, Connecticut, also armed the North.

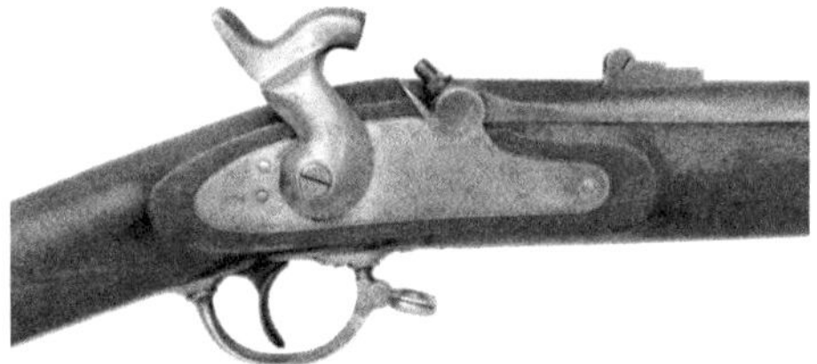

Colt 1861

Hundreds of thousands of these two models of rifles were used by Federal troops and Union state militia in the war. Soldiers of the Confederate States captured many thousands of Springfield and Colt rifles and turned them against the Union. The South also used a number of British weapons purchased early in the war, such as the Enfield rifled musket and the Whitworth target rifle (used for sniper activity).[11]

Post War

After the Civil War, a breech-loading rifle became the primary weapon of the United States Army. This rifle, known as the Springfield "trapdoor" model, used a brass "cartridge" instead of separate powder, bullet, and percussion cap. A type of cartridge had become common for caplock rifles to aid rapid reloading. It had gunpowder encased in paper, with a bullet in one end. The soldier usually tore the bullet end off with his teeth, poured the powder down the rifle barrel, added the paper for wadding, and then used his ramrod to push the bullet down from the muzzle. Once he placed a percussion cap on the nipple, the rifle could be fired. A proficient soldier could do this three or four times in a minute, bringing substantial fire on the enemy.

The term "cartridge" transferred from this paper type for muzzle loaders to the brass version used in breech loaders. The priming compound went into the base, either as part of the rim ("rimfire") or as a separate disc shaped primer in the center of the base ("centerfire"). The "shell" or "case" that held the components was made of brass. Powder filled the hollow interior, and a bullet was "seated" at the open end.

Once the cartridge became secure in the "breech," or back of the barrel, it could be fired by "cocking" the hammer (pulling it back) and pulling the trigger. Cocking placed strong spring tension on the hammer. The trigger pull released or "dropped" the hammer with great force, allowing it to strike the "firing pin." This pin, made of steel, is sometimes a part of the hammer and, as in the trapdoor, sometimes a separate "floating" pin, would impact the rim or primer hard enough to cause the priming to explode.

The resulting flame would ignite the primary powder charge, which would then explode, sending the bullet spinning from the barrel at over 1000 feet per second in the .45-70 caliber cartridge used in most trapdoor rifles. .45 caliber (forty-five one hundredths of an inch) represented the diameter of the bullet. 70 indicated the number of grains (7000 grains = 1 lb.) of powder in the case. The .45-70 was more than powerful enough to kill buffalo, and worked well as a military cartridge.

While the single shot breech loader required several separate motions to load and shoot, it still fired more quickly than a muzzle loader.[12]

Trapdoor

Also available late in the Civil War was the breech loading lever action repeater. It was never assigned as a primary American military weapon; instead, individual officers and soldiers purchased them out of their own pockets.

Lever action rifles had tubular "magazines" under the barrel or in the stock, and were capable of quickly firing up to a dozen or more shots without reloading. The "actions" required a quick, downward motion of the firing hand holding the lever to eject a spent cartridge after each shot, followed by an equally quick upward hand motion to bring a new cartridge from the magazine into the chamber.[13]

Lever Action Model 1886

Western Frontier

Settlers, rangers, hunters, trappers, and other Americans across the West from the Mississippi to the Pacific Ocean frequently carried lever action rifles for self-defense and the defense of their communities. They went armed because they quite reasonably feared the need to defend themselves from attack by Indians, violence by outlaws, and wild animals. A number of different models of lever action repeaters were developed between the 1860s and the late 1800s.

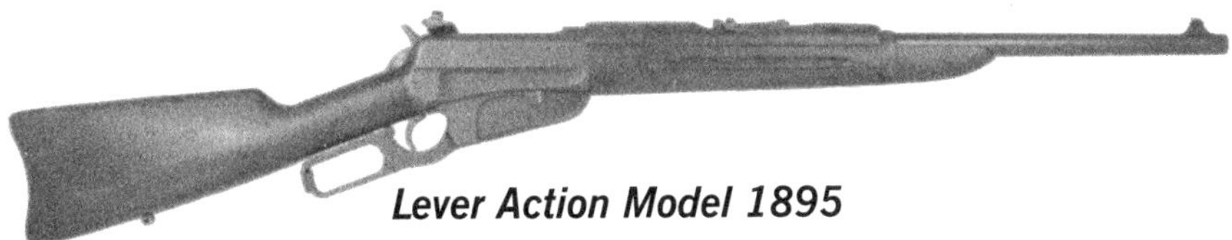
Lever Action Model 1895

Pump action rifles also became available during these years. The front hand gripped a movable forearm attached to the "slide" of the action. The pump required a pulling action to the rear by the front hand, followed by a forward, pushing action with the same hand. It worked as fast or faster than a lever action. Colt called its version of a pump action the "Lightning" because of its extremely fast rate of fire. Lever and pump action rifles first gave individual citizens the rapid firepower needed to overcome attackers when outnumbered. These rifles helped with the taming of the American frontier, which officially closed in 1890.[14]

Spanish American War

A bolt action rifle followed the single shot breech loader as America's next individual military weapon in the 1890s. Wars between the British and the Boers in South Africa, and in the Sudan, with the British and Egyptians fighting the Mahdist armies, first proved the effectiveness of the modern magazine-fed bolt action.[15] The Spanish American War saw U.S. forces using the Krag-Jorgenson .30-40 Krag bolt action rifle.

.30-40 Krag

Military ammunition began to use smokeless powder instead of black powder as its propellant late in the 19th century. This transition caused major changes in weapons, including rifles, as the new smokeless powder reduced the required cleaning of the weapons, and provided an increase in the explosive force, and thus, the power achieved in a given caliber. The changeover was substantially complete by 1906.

Rifles of the American forces in 1898 included the .30-40 Krag bolt action with a smokeless powder in a cartridge of fairly low power, .45-70 trapdoor single shots that still fired black powder, and a variety of personal weapons carried by militia, including lever action rifles. The Spanish had German 7mm Mauser rifles, which proved much more accurate and effective at longer ranges than the U.S. arms. Mauser, a weapons manufacturer, designed both rifles and their ammunition. The 7mm Mauser cartridge used smokeless powder and a .28 caliber bullet that traveled at very high velocity for its time. The U.S. won, despite having the disadvantages of black powder and low powered ammunition.

The War ended on August 12, 1898 and the parties ratified the resulting Treaty of Paris on February 6, 1899. Spanish troops left in

December, 1898 and the U.S. governed Cuba under military occupation until May 20, 1903. The Treaty also ceded the Philippines, Guam, and Puerto Rico to the United States. One of the conditions of the Treaty was for the U.S. to leave Cuba and allow it to become independent in 1903. The agreement also included a perpetual lease by the U.S. of 45 square miles of land and water as a naval base. America still uses this base, called Guantanamo Bay, to this day.

Bolt Action Rifles

The United States purchased rights to the Mauser design, which it modified to make the 1903 Springfield rifle in .30-'03 caliber for United States military use after the Spanish American War.

Springfield 1903

The .30 caliber cartridge was changed to the .30-'06 Springfield with a different powder charge in 1906. This became the primary cartridge used in United States military rifles until well after the Korean War.

The second military bolt action produced for the United States forces in World War I used a British Enfield design. This weapon, known as the pattern 1917, also in .30-'06, provided U.S. troops with rifles made by Winchester, Remington, and Remington's Eddystone factory.

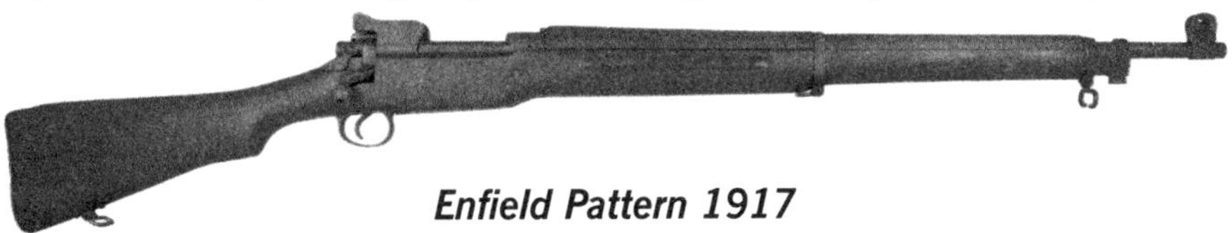

Enfield Pattern 1917

The military continues to use several models of bolt action rifles today, primarily in applications where the inherently superior accuracy of the design takes precedence over a high rate of fire.

Civilian versions of bolt action rifles became very popular in the early 1900s, and their use continues in great numbers for sporting purposes. The sighting system of the Model 1917, an aperture or "peep" sight instead of an open sight, increased accuracy.

1917 Sight

The War Department added this type of sight to the 1903 Springfield after World War I and made some other technical changes to create the model 1903A3 as a primary rifle for the United States military, along with the M-1 Garand, in World War II.

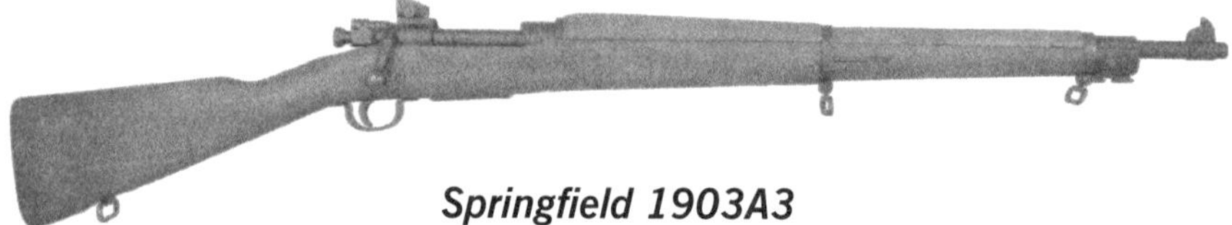

Springfield 1903A3

Aperture sights became standard for all American military rifles, including those in current use.

Between the World Wars

The experience of World War I and the anticipation of future conflicts initiated efforts by the United States to produce a more effective primary battle rifle, which resulted in the production of the M1 Garand starting in 1936. A completely different design using semi-automatic function and a charging clip holding eight rounds, made it an innovative step in military technology. General George S. Patton called it the "greatest single battle implement ever devised by man."[16] Using the same cartridge as the 1903 and 1903A3 models, it fired more rapidly and reloaded more easily. The firepower of eight rounds fired semi-automatically (one shot for each trigger pull) as opposed to the usual five in the magazine of a bolt action rifle, which required manual rechambering for each shot, gave individual soldiers an important advantage over their enemies.

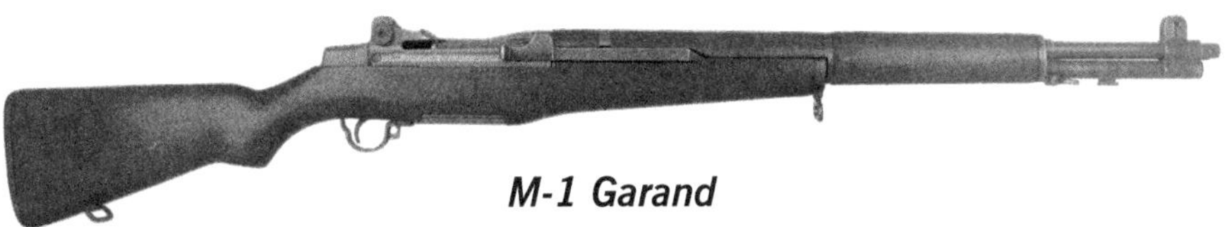

M-1 Garand

The bolt action rifle requires holding or bracing with one hand while operating the bolt to chamber a cartridge (also known as a "round") with the other. This action must be repeated after each shot to eject the spent brass and move a new round from the rifle's magazine to its chamber. Called rechambering, this process continues until the magazine "goes dry" or empties, after which it must be reloaded. The action of a semi-automatic rifle uses the energy of a fired cartridge to "cycle" the action instantly after the trigger pull, so that the spent brass ejects and a new round chambers instantaneously, without further effort from the shooter.

The M-1 carbine, another innovative firearm developed in the United States during the 1930s, was designed and used to arm soldiers who would otherwise have carried only a pistol. The .30 carbine cartridge has a higher velocity and more energy than the .45 caliber pistol cartridge, and its shoulder stock, longer barrel and aperture sights gave it much better accuracy. In World War II, the magazine held 15 rounds, and could be changed quickly.

M-1 carbine

The use of semi-automatic rifles for sporting purposes became much more common after World War II. Millions of former military members had trained with and become comfortable shooting the semi-automatic M-1 Garand and M-1 carbine. Winchester, Remington, Harrington and Richardson, Browning, and other rifle manufacturers released a variety of semi-automatic hunting rifles in large numbers. Many fired the .30-'06 Springfield caliber due to the ready availability of ammunition and widespread familiarity with the cartridge.

Remington 7400

The Korean War saw the introduction of one new small arm to the American military. Based upon the M-1 carbine, the new M-2 carbine had a modified action that allowed it to work as a full automatic.[17] Adding a 30 round magazine for more capacity, it still used the .30 carbine cartridge.

.45 ACP, .30 Carbine, and 9mm

The M-2 carbine could not be transferred to civilians because of the National Firearms Act, but the M-1 carbine remained a very popular sporting and self-defense rifle after the war.

M-1 Carbine Closeup

The bolt action rifle saw much less use by the Korean War. Most of the approximately 3 million citizen soldiers trained with and carried the semi-automatic M-1 Garand. The U.S. Army looked at its weapons after the Korean War and decided to replace the M-1 Garand, the M-2 carbine and the BAR with a single rifle, the M-14. This rifle used a new, shorter .30 caliber cartridge designated the 7.62 NATO (.308 Winchester). A new machine gun, the M-60, used the same cartridge on belts.

America's Military Rifle Cartridges, from 1873 to Present

The U.S. Military's primary weapon at the beginning of the Vietnam conflict was the M-14.

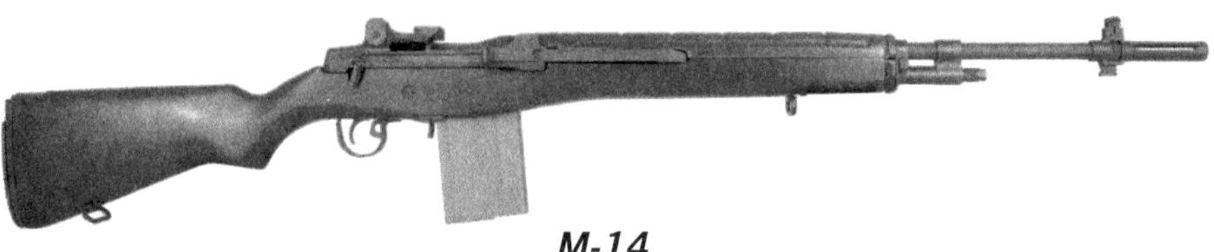

M-14

A model without the full automatic option, called the M-1A, became the civilian counterpart.

Both the M-14 and M-1A still see use today by military and civilians. The long range engagement distances in Afghanistan have caused the military to return to the M-14 in some units. Civilian Marksmanship Program training and competitions have continued with the M-1A since its introduction.

M-1A

The M-1A fits the usual role as the civilian version of a common military rifle.

Sniper Rifles

The military has had snipers from the very beginning of our history. The Kentucky or Pennsylvania flintlock rifle frequently saw use as a sniper weapon from the Indian Wars through the War of 1812. Civilian caplocks and target rifles were common tools of snipers during the Civil War. Purpose-built sniper rifles have seen combat use by American forces from World War I through the recent wars of the early 21st century.

During World War II, the German, Japanese, and Russians trained snipers for long-range accurate fire to harass the enemies and kill important targets, such as officers and gunners. The United States conducted a similar program in World War II, using the bolt action rifle of World War I, with telescopic sights added. Later in the war, it also developed a sniper version of the M1 Garand with a telescopic sight. U.S. military sniper rifles of World War II and Korea fired .30-'06 caliber ammunition. Civilians had long used telescopic sights ("scopes") mounted on similar sporting rifles for hunting purposes.

1903 Sporter

With the introduction of the 7.62 NATO (or .308 Winchester) for the M-14, sniper rifles began to change to that caliber. American Bolt action rifles with telescopic sights in 7.62 NATO have seen extensive service from Vietnam in the late 1960s to Iraq and Afghanistan. M-14s can also serve as sniper rifles when accurized and scoped. The .308 Winchester (7.62 NATO) cartridge has become one of the most popular rounds for civilian hunting and competition in both bolt action and semi-auto models.

The military began to use the M-16 rifle early in the Vietnam War (1965-1972). Special operations forces and paratroopers carried M-16s because the light weight and smaller cartridge allowed them to carry additional ammunition and equipment. When the war began, most soldiers and Marines carried the M-14. This changed steadily, and by the late 1960s nearly all U.S. units had the M-16 or M-16A1 as their primary rifle.[18]

The next chapter on modern arms will discuss the M-16 in more detail, including a description of its role as America's first true assault rifle. That chapter will also explain the differences between the M-16 and the AR-15, its very popular (and also much maligned) civilian counterpart.

Chapter 6

MODERN ARMS

Service Rifles, Assault Weapons, and Bans

The "old soldiers" who taught me about rifles scoffed at the M-16. They thought that its plastic stock and .22 caliber cartridge bordered upon silliness. Mostly combat veterans and law enforcement officers, they believed that battle rifles should have far more range and penetration capability than the M-16. The small, lightweight modern weapon also seemed unsuitable for close quarters combat with bayonet and rifle butt. It reminded them of the M-1 Carbine, which they universally despised.

Before going to college in 1974, I saw the M-16 only on the TV news. My father watched Walter Cronkite on CBS whenever possible, and his coverage of the Vietnam War, which dominated the news in the late '60s and early '70s, often showed M-16s in action.

My first hands-on experience with the M-16 came with R.O.T.C. classes at the College of William and Mary. The U.S. Army had graciously awarded me a four-year Army R.O.T.C. scholarship, and I became extremely familiar with M-16s as a result.

After what seemed at the time an extraordinary amount of classroom training on the rifle, my class finally went to Fort Eustis at Newport News, Virginia for live fire training and qualification. I found the M-16 extremely easy to shoot and qualified as "Expert." I fired M-16s for qualification 14 more times during my military service, each time qualifying as "Expert."

Everyone in the Army learned to field strip and take care of the M-16. We also received some basic marksmanship instruction in classroom settings. All of us drilled and marched with the rifle, as well as literally living with it for weeks at a time in the field. Qualification involved "zeroing" the M-16 at short range to confirm that the sights functioned properly, then shooting a "course of fire."

The courses of fire, ranges, and requirements have changed several times since the 1970s, but the concept remains similar. The soldier fires a number of rounds (now 40) from various positions at different ranges. Ranges changed from 50 meters to 300 meters in 50 meter increments. The "Firer" now has to make at least 36 out of 40 verified hits to qualify as "Expert."

I decided that my relatives and my father's friends had misjudged the rifle, at least as a short and medium-range weapon. The military obviously agreed, since the Army and Navy have issued versions of the M-16 to soldiers and Marines for more than half a century. The M-16, in part due to the popularity of its civilian counterpart, the AR-15, has become America's very popular service rifle.

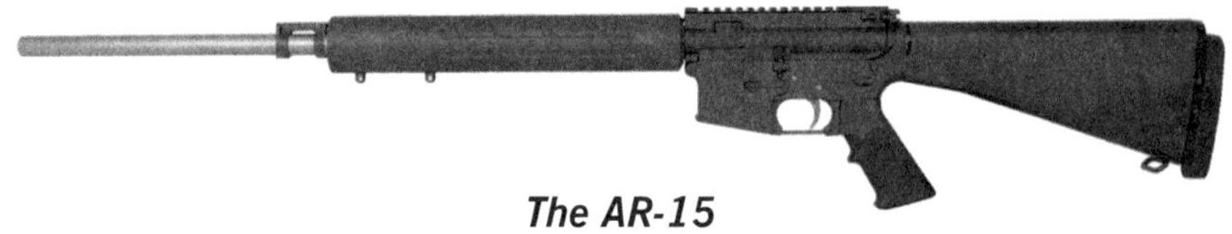

The AR-15

In addition to carrying an M-16 as my assigned weapon for untold hours and firing it during training and for qualification, I learned about it from a Range Officer's point of view. Once my active duty requirements and some other assignments ended, I served for nine years as a "citizen soldier" in the 1st Battalion, 116th Infantry, 29th Infantry Division of the Virginia Army National Guard. During several of those years I had duty as the Officer in Charge (OIC) of M-16 qualification ranges.

I supervised rifle ranges with up to 100 firing points on multiple occasions at Fort Pickett near Blackstone, Virginia, Fort A.P. Hill at Bowling Green, Virginia and at Fort Bragg outside Fayetteville, North Carolina. These experiences showed me the versatility of an M-16 for use by soldiers with all levels of physical capabilities and skill.

M-16 Characteristics

M-16s and AR-15s have several common characteristics that make them easy to shoot accurately. First and foremost, the extremely mild recoil of the 5.56 NATO (.223 Remington) cartridge allows virtually painless firing by anyone. The recoil from rifles chambered in other military calibers, like the 7.62 NATO (.308 Winchester) and .30-'06 Springfield often hurt the shooter's shoulder. It takes tough shoulder muscles and extensive practice to comfortably shoot the larger caliber rounds without flinching in anticipation of their more violent recoil. With the minimal recoil management needed to fire an M-16, those learning to shoot it can focus on other marksmanship skills, like sight picture and trigger control.

Low recoil makes holding the sights on target for the split second after the trigger is pulled a simple accomplishment. It is called "follow through," and shooters find this basic requirement for accurate shooting very hard to meet when their rifles painfully "kick" their shoulders with every squeeze of the trigger.

Each qualification range I managed would see my NCOs (non-commissioned officers, usually sergeants) and I process from 200 to 400 soldiers on the firing line. Sometimes this took two days. We started shortly after daylight and fired until dusk. We occasionally finished the qualification process early and had both time and excess ammunition available. No ammunition supply point (ASP) wanted returned ammunition, so my NCOs and I had a chance to practice. We shot at all distances and often fired on "full-auto" until the ammo ran out. Qualification never included full-auto fire. This avoided the ammo turn-in problem, and enabled us to learn how to accurately place fully automatic fire.

Automatic Fire

The fundamental differences between the M-16 and the AR-15 relate to the M-16's ability to achieve fully automatic fire. M-16s have autosears, trigger disconnects, different triggers, and different hammers than AR-15s. The AR-15 also has design features that prevent its conversion to fully automatic operation. For example, AR-15s come with bolts and receivers that will not work with the parts that permit full automatic fire.

Marksmen learning to fire the M-16 on full-auto require different training than they need when learning the semi-auto AR-15. They must manage burst fire, learn muzzle control, stay aware of barrel temperature, and carefully watch ammunition usage.

A burst occurs when the shooter pulls the trigger of a full-auto and it fires several rounds (usually three) at once. The energy from firing several rounds in a burst causes the rifle's muzzle (front end) to rise or jump, which takes some skill to control. If full-auto fire continues at too high a rate, the rifle barrel will overheat and the rifle will malfunction. Ammunition runs out very quickly during full-auto fire, so shooters have to stay aware of its availability.

The full automatic feature of the M-16 allows a soldier to effectively fire up to 200 rounds per minute, using short bursts. A civilian AR-15 has an effective fire rate of about 65 rounds per minute.[1]

The civilian AR-15 has become one of the most controversial firearms in American history. Its use by mentally ill individuals to commit horrible killings, such as at Sandy Hook and Aurora, has fueled the controversy. The words used to describe it show the wide variety of attitudes toward these rifles.

The political left calls the AR-15 a "Killing Machine" (CNN), "Weapon of War" (President Obama), or an "Assault Weapon" (most Democrats). Many citizens call it a Target Rifle (casual target shooters), "Varmint Rifle" (most hunters) or a "self-defense rifle." Competition shooters call their version a "match rifle." The Civilian Marksmanship Program (CMP) terms the AR-15 a "Service Rifle." The National Rifle Association (NRA) prefers "Modern Sporting Rifle."

The military M-16 goes by "Individual Weapon" or "Rifle," but never "gun." Simply using the term "AR-15" lets the military differentiate the modern full-auto M-16 from its semi-auto counterpart. M-16s also fit the traditional military definition of an "Assault Rifle." The military calls the compact version of the M-16 an M-4.

The M-4

Assault Weapons

The military term "assault rifle" and the political term "assault weapon" have very little in common. Assault rifle refers to a design that includes specific characteristics, such as detachable magazines, full automatic capability, lower recoil rifle ammunition, and bayonet attachments.

"Assault weapon" seems a value judgment assigned by politicians to firearms they do not want citizens to have. It goes with the argument that weapons "designed for war" should not have Second Amendment protections. Each law that bans such assault weapons includes a statutory definition. The laws vary from describing certain characteristics to listing specific firearms by make and model.

Most assault weapon statutes include a variety of pistols and shotguns in their definitions, as well as semi-automatic rifles.

Assault Rifles

Germany pioneered the concept with its MP-43 during World War II. This rifle used a shortened rifle cartridge, the 8mm Kurtz (short) derived from the standard 8mm Mauser (.32 caliber). It had the ability to fire as a semi-automatic or full automatic. Renamed the "Sturmgewehr" (German for assault rifle) in 1944, it used a 30 round detachable magazine. While not a long range weapon, it provided devastating fire power at close and medium ranges.

A Russian named Mikhail Kalashnikov designed a similar rifle shortly after World War II. Called the AK-47 (Avtomat Kalashnikova), it fired a short 7.62 x 39mm rifle cartridge (.30 caliber) and became the most common assault rifle throughout the Eastern bloc communist countries and much of the Third World. Most other countries with weapons manufacturing capabilities also produced assault rifles of some type in the 1950s and after.

The U.S. military did not have an effective assault rifle until the introduction of the M-14. Despite the full automatic capability and 30 round magazine of the U.S. M-2 carbine, it proved an ineffective assault rifle due to its relatively under-powered .30 caliber pistol cartridge. The Browning Automatic Rifle (BAR) weighed too much and fired the full length .30-'06, although it had a 20 round detachable box magazine. M-1 Garands, also firing the .30-'06, held only eight shots in a fixed magazine. After the Korean War, the United States military realized that it needed an assault rifle to replace all three of these weapons.

The M-14 filled this role, but it proved unwieldy and difficult to handle for some members of the military because of its relatively high-powered 7.62 x 51mm (.308 Win.) ammunition, its 46-1/2" length, and its 11-1/2 pound weight. Many soldiers had trouble with the recoil, especially when firing on full automatic. The M-16/AR-15 family of rifles gradually replaced the M-14 as the individual weapon of the U.S. military, between the late 1960s and early 1980s. While the ammunition used by the M-16, 5.56 NATO, has very little recoil, its velocity (over 3,000 feet per second) gives the fairly small 5.56mm (.22 caliber) bullet enough energy for effective military use in most situations. The smaller (roughly 39-5/8") size and lower (slightly less than 6-1/2 pound) weight of the rifle and its less bulky ammunition allowed a person armed with an M-16 to carry more than twice as many rounds of ammo as someone assigned an M-14.

Service Rifles

Now the M-16 rifle (in one of its later variations) arms most of the American military as the standard "service rifle." Learning about and firing the M-16 are common experiences for all who have served in the United States military over the last 40 years. Millions of private citizens legally own AR-15s for defense, hunting, target practice, and competition shooting.[2]

The Federal government began encouraging and organizing civilian marksmanship training and competition shooting with the War Department Appropriations Act of 1903. Surplus rifles became available for purchase by civilians through the Army in 1905. The Civilian Marksmanship Program continues to sell surplus rifles today under the Federal statute that preceded the 1905 law. The Army and the National Rifle Association jointly organized service rifle training for young men (women were not included in the early 1900s), and assisted with nationwide local competitive shooting matches, as well as an annual National Match as part of the Civilian Marksmanship Program (CMP).[3]

The U.S. government under Theodore Roosevelt wanted American civilians to become familiar with and practice with the new national service rifle, the bolt-action 1903 Springfield. Service rifles (a standard issue military rifle or civilian equivalent) appropriate under the Second Amendment for civilian ownership fell into two categories. First were those which had become obsolete and no longer served as military weapons. The 1903 Springfield and 1917 Enfield fit this definition perfectly after World War II because by then the 1903A3 and M1 Garand replaced them for use by U.S. soldiers and Marines. The second category of citizen arms included a variety of rifle models that had never been issued as standard for U.S. government forces, but had some features of military rifles. Kentucky rifles and lever actions exemplified this type, as did bolt action sporters and, currently, the more modern civilian versions of military service rifles.

Attempts to eliminate the Civilian Marksmanship Program in 1996 failed when lawmakers who supported national marksmanship training prevented its complete repeal. However, Congress ended Army responsibility for operating the CMP, though the military continues to provide logistical support for competitions and activities. The Army also assigns National Guard or Reserve soldiers to support national matches, which continue to be held at Department of Defense facilities. The Army still provides surplus rifles and ammunition to the CMP for civilian use. Today, the nonprofit "Corporation for The Promotion of Rifle Practice and Firearms Safety" manages the CMP, operating under Federal law.[4]

The CMP continues to provide training, practice, and competitions for Americans using service rifles and pistols. It holds annual National Matches and Game Events at Camp Perry in Ohio. The matches and games include both military and civilian participants. Game events include Garand, Springfield (1903 and 1903A3 models), M-1 Carbine and "Military Rifle." CMP Competition Rules for Service Rifle and Service Pistol allow competition with three specific service rifles in the Military Rifle matches.[5]

Section 6.1, "General Service Rifle Rules," sets out the requirements:

> *6.2.1 U.S. Rifle, Caliber .30, M-1 – The Rifle must be a rifle that was issued by the U. S. Armed Forces or a commercial rifle of the same type and caliber (Garand).*
>
> *6.2.2 U.S. Rifle, Caliber 7.62 NATO (.308Win) M-14 – The rifle must*

be a rifle that was issued by the U.S. Armed Forces or a commercial rifle of the same type and caliber (M-1A).

6.2.3 U.S. Rifle, Caliber 5.56mm, M-16 – The rifle must be an M-16A2 or M-16A4 rifle issued by the U.S. Armed Forces or a Commercial rifle of the same type and caliber (AR-15).

The CMP still sells surplus military rifles, except for the M-14 and M-16, because the National Firearms Act prevents sale to non-government owners due to their full-auto capability. Recent CMP sales include the .30-40 Krag, 1903, 1917, 1903A3, M-1 Carbine, and M-1 Garand. The CMP also sells standard U.S. ammunition, such as .22 Long Rifle rimfire target loads, 5.56mm, .30 Carbine, 7.62mm, and .30-'06.

While the CMP does not sell the M-1A or AR-15, private vendors frequently sell these rifles at matches, in an area called "commercial row." Manufacturers, custom gun makers, and others with the appropriate licenses can sell match quality semi-auto service rifles to civilians at CMP functions.

Future sales of surplus rifles by the CMP are in doubt because President Obama has blocked their import by executive action.[6] The action primarily effects recovery of M-1 Garands and M-1 Carbines from allies, South Korea, for example. Federal law authorizes recovering surplus firearms, but the officials who implement the law work for the executive branch.[7] When the CMP exhausts its current inventory, future sales will have to wait for a new administration.

Assault Weapon Bans

I frequently hear outrage from acquaintances and gun show attendees about public officials who have sworn to protect, defend and uphold the Constitution, yet continue to work hard to pass laws that violate it. Assault weapon bans proposed and sometimes passed in the face of the Second Amendment provide clear examples, especially those bans that targeted the AR-15.

Nine states and Washington, D.C. have passed assault weapon bans that "infringe" upon rights to "keep and bear" the civilian service rifle. The Obama administration and liberal lawmakers continue to aggressively pursue enactment of a similar Federal ban. Several State Supreme Courts and lower Federal courts have upheld these laws.

AR-15 Bans

President Obama promotes banning the AR-15 and its magazines as one of his "common-sense" gun control measures.[8] Given his comments about America's gun laws becoming like those of England and Australia, the President must see an assault weapon ban as a step on the path to complete civilian disarmament. Most of the President's arguments for banning the AR-15 defy Supreme Court rulings.

One argument for banning the AR-15 claims that our founders did not envision modern weapons, and therefore, the Second Amendment should not apply to those weapons. The Supreme Court addressed that contention as follows: "Some have made the argument, bordering on the frivolous, that only those arms in existence in the 18th century are protected by the Second Amendment. We do not interpret constitutional rights that way. Just as the First Amendment affects modern forms of communications and the Fourth Amendment applies to modern forms of search, the Second Amendment extends, *prima facie*, to all instruments that constitute bearable arms, even those that were not existent at the time of the founding."[9] The court goes on to explain that the right to keep arms applies to everyone and not simply to members of a military organization.[10]

A different argument, often used by the President, asserts that even one life saved is worth giving up Second Amendment rights. This "interest-balancing" approach with respect to the Second Amendment elicited the following response from the Supreme Court:

> *"We know of no other enumerated constitutional rights whose core protection has been subjected to a free standing 'interest-balancing' approach. The very enumeration of the rights takes out of the hands of government ... even the third branch of government ... the power to decide on a case by case basis whether the right is really worth insisting upon. A constitutional guarantee subject to future judges' assessments of its usefulness is no constitutional guarantee at all. Constitutional rights are enshrined with the scope they were understood to have when the people adopted them, whether or not future legislatures or (yes) even future judges think that scope is too broad. We would not apply an interest-balancing approach to the prohibition of a peaceful neo-Nazi march through Skokie. The First Amendment contains the freedom-of-speech guarantee that the people ratified, which*

include exceptions for obscenity, libel, and disclosure of state secrets, but not for the expression of extremely unpopular and wrong-headed views. The Second Amendment is no different."[11]

The Common Defense

President Obama and others who would ban AR-15s constantly refer to them as "military style weapons" or "weapons of war" as if these labels somehow make their argument. But the main reason for the Second Amendment involves civilian ownership of firearms suitable as weapons for war in a crisis. The logical "arm" for citizens to "bear" in case of a call to service seems the civilian version of the current service rifle, or the AR-15. With the concept of a civilian militia available for defense of both themselves and their community at the core of the Second Amendment, it must also include ammunition, magazines and other equipment needed for effective defense. Bans that "infringe" upon the possession and use of these "arms" ignore the Constitution.

Another argument for bans claims that Americans can rely upon government forces for defense and no foreseeable need exists for citizens to possess arms for the common defense. As earlier chapters set out in detail, it takes a remarkable lack of imagination to believe this argument. Standing ready for the unexpected has deep roots as an American tradition.

The founders of the United States included the Second Amendment in the Bill of Rights and considered the right to keep and bear arms essential for the liberty of America's people.[12] But the anti-gun movement believes that citizens no longer need arms for defense of their liberty and should surrender them in the name of "gun violence prevention."

All these arguments for banning the AR-15 call for challenging or outright ignoring the Constitution. Consider the relevant words: "We the people of the United States, in order to form a more perfect Union, establish Justice, insure domestic Tranquility, provide for the common defense, promote the general Welfare, and secure the Blessing of Liberty to ourselves and our Posterity do ordain [that]...the right of the people to keep and bear arms shall not be infringed." The U.S. Supreme Court in *U.S. v. Miller* and *D.C. v. Heller* confirmed that citizens have the right to keep and bear the kinds of arms in common use now, the use of which could contribute to the common defense.[13] As the very popular civilian version of our widely used military rifle, the AR-15 serves as the ideal rifle for Americans to have for the Second Amendment purpose of common defense.

Protection and security from attack or invasion by foreign powers, violence from other citizens, insurrection, and other activities endangering public safety constitute the common defense. Common defense encompasses defending neighborhoods, communities, cities, counties, states, and the nation. Or in other words, collective self-defense. Self preservation and defense of family logically come first for individuals, with collective or common defense becoming even more important when the threat defended against exceeds the ability of individuals to face alone.

Changing the Constitution

Under the United States' system of government, we have only one appropriate method of reversing the decision by our founders to include the right to bear arms in our Constitution; neither the Legislative Branch, the Executive Branch, nor the courts should dispense with or change the meaning of the Second Amendment. The Supreme Court said in the closing lines of the *Heller* opinion: "Undoubtedly some think that the Second Amendment is outmoded in a society where our standing army is the pride of our nation, where well trained police forces provide personal security, and where gun violence is a serious problem. That is perhaps debatable, but what is not debatable is that it is not the role of this Court to pronounce the Second Amendment extinct."[14]

The Constitution itself provides the mechanism for changing the Second Amendment. Under Article 5, it says: "The Congress, whenever two-thirds of both houses shall deem it necessary, shall propose amendments to this Constitution, or, on the application of the legislatures of two-thirds of the several states, shall call a convention for proposing amendments, which, in either case, shall be valid to all intents and purposes, as part of this Constitution, when ratified by the legislatures of three-fourths of the several states, or by conventions in three-fourths thereof, as the one or other mode of ratification may be proposed by the Congress."

If the American people no longer believe they need a right to keep and bear arms for common defense and the preservation of liberty they can amend the Constitution to repeal or alter the Second Amendment.

Activist Courts

The Constitution has not changed, and everyone who knows anything about the subject considers the AR-15 America's civilian service rifle. Yet states and cities have banned it, obviously infringing upon the right to keep and bear it. How do these lawmakers get away with what seems such a clear violation of the Constitution? The answer comes from the courts that have upheld some of these bans.

Ban advocates put forth the proposition that the AR-15 and similar weapons fall within the Supreme Court discussion of "dangerous and unusual weapons," ownership of which can be prohibited or "infringed" upon under the Constitution.

The *Heller* court stated: "We also recognize another important limitation on the right to keep and carry arms. *Miller* said, as we have explained, that the sorts of weapons protected were those *in common use at the time.*[15] We think that limitation is fairly supported by the historical tradition of prohibiting the carrying of 'dangerous and unusual weapons.'"[16]

California's highest court ruled in 2009 that the Second Amendment does not protect the right of citizens to keep and bear the AR-15.[17] The law in question, the state's, Assault Weapons Control Act of 1989, bans the AR-15 by name in its list of "assault weapons."[18] The James case opinion declares that…"the Second Amendment…does not protect the right to possess assault weapons."[19]

The judges allege "the fact that assault weapons, like machine guns, are not in common use by law-abiding citizens for lawful purposes and likewise fall within the category of dangerous and unusual weapons that the government can prohibit for individual use."[20] The fact of the AR15's widespread popularity among and use for lawful purposes by millions of law-abiding citizens would seem to counter this assertion quite effectively.

The United States Court of Appeals for the District of Columbia also upheld a law prohibiting "assault weapons" and magazines holding over ten rounds. That court, in another case involving Mr. Heller as a party, considered a law enacted by the D.C. Council. The decision, known as *Heller II*, was handed down on October 4, 2011. Two of the three judges said that because the ban did not meaningfully affect individual self-defense, its prohibitions are constitutional.

The D.C. judges focus on self-defense in the home as the "central component" or "core purpose" of the Second Amendment. They rely on some of the language of the Supreme Court in the original *Heller* case to reach this ruling. The court in *Heller II* simply ignores large portions of the first *Heller* case with respect to common defense and the preservation of liberty. It also accepts as fact the assertions of the D.C. Council's Committee on Public Safety report that AR-15s, as "military-style" weapons designed only for offensive use, have no useful purpose for sport or self-defense. The *Heller II* court then "balances" the D.C. government's interests against those of private citizens and rules in favor of the Government.

But what about the U.S. Supreme Court? Surely it will follow its own precedent and correctly find that the Constitution protects the right of citizens to keep and bear America's civilian service rifle. I believe so, with the current Justices. But what if one or more of the probable majority leaves the Court?

A number of Supreme Court cases have been decided with a 5 - 4 margin in recent years. The usual majority, Justices Scalia, Kennedy, Thomas, Roberts, and Alito, are relatively conservative Justices who tend in most cases to follow the Constitution as written and interpreted by prior Supreme Court cases. The minority, Justices Kagan, Ginsburg, Breyer, and Sotomayor, are more likely to change meaning or overturn prior cases to reach a desired result.

In a different context, the *Wall Street Journal* discusses this subject and makes this statement: "The truth is that the High Court is one vote away from a liberal lockstep majority that is dangerous to American self-defense."[21]

Speaking of assault weapons bans that violate the Second Amendment, as set forth in *Heller*, the *Wall Street Journal* speculates that "Part of the liberal calculations here may be that *Heller* was decided 5-4, so only a single change of mind is needed to make a gun ban constitutional. Justice Ruth Bader Ginsburg (a dissenter in *Heller*) has gone so far as to suggest publicly that a "future, wise court" might reconsider the ruling.[22]

So no matter how clear the issue of whether the AR-15 can be "banned" under the Second Amendment may seem, the courts can rule either way. The effort to "ban" requires characterizing semi-automatic rifles as both "dangerous" and "unusual," so that they may be treated the same way as destructive devices and machine guns under the law. Acceptance of such a characterization also means accepting that the Second Amendment does not apply to collective self-defense and securing liberty.

Senate Democrats voted on November 21, 2013 to alter a 225-year-old Senate procedure in what many call the "nuclear option" of rule changes. "The rule change allows nominations to proceed with 51 votes, down from the 60-vote threshold that had long applied."[23] Apparently done at the request of President Obama,[24] "the change gives Mr. Obama more flexibility to shape the federal judiciary."[25]

We can expect a large number of new Federal judges with policy preferences that generally mirror the President's positions on all aspects of the Constitution, including the Second Amendment. Judges have a number of ways to find in favor of the side that reflects their preferences.

For example, they can make findings of fact which tend to support the preferred result, like the acceptance in *Heller II* of the purported status of AR-15s as "unusual." They can also apply different levels of scrutiny to avoid strict application of the Constitution, again as in *Heller II*.

When looking at the constitutionality of bans, judges can defer to the constitutional assessments of the legislators who wrote the ban laws, or restrain themselves from judicial interference with legislation. The legal community calls these approaches "the doctrines of deference and restraint."[26] Legislators then turn around and rely on the court's willingness to uphold their powers as proof of their constitutionality."[27]

"With judges deferring to legislatures and vice versa, no one actually enforces the Constitution's constraints on legislative powers."[28]

Conclusion

Along with progressive, activist judges, a number of government employees, many politicians, a substantial part of the American population, and much of the international community want to see private citizens disarmed. Another large portion of the people and their representatives strongly believe that the individual American's right to bear arms has a crucial place in our future, and not only for defense in the home. The effort to disarm, with a few interruptions, began in the 1960s and continues today.

The arming of the American people started with our earliest history, and continues today. The bitter political conflict over this subject seems endless. The legal answer to the conflict under our Constitution could turn upon the definition of "militia," discussed at length in the next chapter.

Chapter 7

MILITIA

America's Citizen Soldiers

America's birth involved an almost constant state of war. Survival required proficiency with firearms and the participation in community defense by every able-bodied citizen. Beginning with the first permanent settlement at Jamestown, colonists needed weapons to protect themselves not only from predatory animals, but from violent attacks by Indians, pirates, criminals, foreign invaders, and, ultimately, the forces of their own rulers.

The Second Amendment clearly enshrines this tradition in the Constitution. Suggestions that the right to bear arms applies only to sports and home defense simply defy the reality of history. Citizens had weapons or arms suitable for war and the rights they insisted upon in the Constitution include the right to keep and bear those arms.

The Oxford Dictionary of American English defines "Militia" as "a military force that is raised from the civil population to supplement a regular army in an emergency" or, alternatively, "all able-bodied civilians eligible by law for military service."[1] The history and laws of the United States confirm these definitions. The Supreme Court in *Heller* said, "the militia comprise all males physically capable of acting in concert for the common defense."[2]

Colonial Indian Wars

Throughout the 1600s, American colonists experienced constant conflict with Indians. The "Anglo-Indian Wars" in Virginia occurred during three distinct time periods, the first beginning in 1609 and ending in 1614. The second Anglo-Indian war took place from 1622 to 1632. The third started in 1644 and ended in 1646.

Throughout all of these wars, the entire male population of the Virginia Colony served as either soldiers or militia. The militia used personal weapons or matchlocks and other arms sent by the Crown for Colony defense. Skirmishes and battles with the Indians continued throughout the century, with the colonists organizing themselves as militia and reorganizing on more than one occasion.

In 1684, a Virginia statute commanded all colonists to obtain personal arms for use as militia. This statute lapsed for a time when the frontier garrisons were disbanded. However, the Colony reenacted the law in 1690, establishing garrisons of rangers to protect the frontier due to fears of further violence from Indians. The governor made visits throughout Virginia to muster men, instruct them via military training exercises, and conduct inspections of arms. During 1694, the new governor, Edmund Andros, "reincorporated the entire populous [sic] into the militia" and "ordered that they be instructed in military tactics, reasoning that in times of need the entire militia should be knowledgeable in the art of war."[3]

The Anglo-Indian wars of Virginia only hint at the extent of the colonial wars in British North America. The New England area suffered several vicious wars, as did New York, New Jersey, and the Carolinas. English settlers first arrived in Massachusetts in 1620, and others soon followed to settle much of the northeast. The Pequot War of 1634-1638 involved the defense of settlements on the Massachusetts Bay, Connecticut River, and Hudson River by Puritan militia of the Massachusetts and Connecticut Colonies. These militiamen would have been armed with matchlock and possibly a few flintlock muskets and wheellocks.

During "King Phillip's War" of 1675-1678, about half of all New England communities had to defend against Indian attacks, and twelve towns were completely destroyed. The Indians killed over 600 colonists, but ultimately lost to the militias of Massachusetts, Connecticut, and present day Rhode Island. By the late 1600s, many more flintlock muskets were used by the militia.

New France and New England fought each other in "King William's War" from 1688 to 1697. Europeans called the territory claimed by the French in 17th century North America "New France." "Queen Anne's War" involved Indians, the Spanish, and the French, fighting against New England and the Carolinas, beginning in 1702 and ending in 1713. French and Indians fought New England again from 1722 to 1725 in "Father Rale's War." Another war with French and Indians, "King George's War," included battles in New York, Massachusetts, and New Hampshire, starting in 1744 and continuing until 1748. "Father LeLoutre's War" of 1749 to 1754 saw a French Catholic priest leading Indians to attack British Protestants in New England. All of these wars forced colonial militiamen to defend their homes and communities, usually with flintlock muskets.

French and Indian War

A company of Virginia militia under Lieutenant Colonel George Washington fought the opening battle of the French and Indian War over construction of a British fort at the "Forks of the Ohio" in Pennsylvania. Throughout the war, from 1754 to 1763, colonial militiamen used privately owned muskets and rifles to defend their homes from raids and participate in battles. Hundreds of militia from Virginia, Maryland, and the Carolinas supplemented British regulars fighting French and Indians at the Battle of the Monongahela on July 9, 1755.[4]

Massachusetts sent 800 militia to reinforce the regulars defending Fort William Henry in 1757. British forces at the Battle of Carillon consisted of eight regiments of regulars and six regiments of militia in 1758. The Battle of Ticonderoga, also in 1758, included militia regiments from New York, Massachusetts, Rhode Island, Connecticut, and New Jersey. Each regiment typically held several hundred men. Colonial militia forces (also called "Provincials") helped British regulars fight the French at the 1759 Battle of Niagara.[5]

American Revolution

During the American Revolution, flintlock rifles in the hands of militia proved deadly additions to the battlefield. "For careful, aimed shooting they were supreme and were responsible for raising the casualty rate among the British and Hessian officers."[6]

The Massachusetts militia opposed 1,800 British troops in the first battle of the American Revolution near Boston. British commanders sent a force to seize weapons and ammunition at the Massachusetts Colony's Concord armory on April 19, 1775. The militia resisted, fighting a pitched battle in the village of Lexington and harassing the British as they retreated back to Boston. The British regulars lost 269 men, and

90 militiamen died. There is no reliable record of how many militiamen participated in the battle.

In the next armed conflict of the Revolution, the Battle of Bunker Hill, on June 17, 1775, the militia of Massachusetts, Connecticut, and New Hampshire, equipped with an assortment of muskets, rifles, and other arms, faced intense cannon fire from the British Navy, as well as a ground assault by over 2,000 British regular soldiers. Militia with muskets stood in ranks behind earthworks, walls, and fences on Breed's Hill, adjacent to Bunker Hill, taking turns firing and reloading to repulse repeated British attacks.

Marksmen in the militia focused on targeting British officers, with deadly success. British Marine Lieutenant John Clarke saw one militiaman kill at least twenty British officers in about ten minutes by having loaded muskets handed to him by other defenders after each of his shots.[7]

The British reformed and attacked yet again, this time bringing cannon forward in support. Despite severe losses, the regulars pushed into the defenders' ranks, finally defeating the militia. The fight, which lasted less than an hour and a half, resulted in 420 American casualties and 1,054 British casualties.

With the loss of half of their attacking force, the British found the price of victory extremely high. They also discovered the militia's unexpected ability to stand and fight against trained regular troops. The British ultimately abandoned Boston to the Americans in March of 1776, when they found themselves faced with cannons placed on the heights above Boston. Their planned attack to dislodge the cannon from the heights did not occur, in part due to the fear of "another Bunker Hill or worse."[8]

Three brigades of Virginia militia helped defeat the British at the Revolution's final Battle of Yorktown. "The back country riflemen carried long, small caliber rifles, weapons of considerably greater accuracy than the ordinary musket and which their owners used with proficiency."[9]

Out of ammunition and lacking bayonets, the Americans at Bunker Hill had no way to repel the British regulars when they closed in to continue the fight with bayonets attached to "Brown Bess" muskets.

The militia who did not leave the field were stabbed and clubbed to death by British soldiers trained in close quarters combat. Despite these disadvantages, the militia forces were critical to the Colonies' success in nearly every battle of their bid for independence.

United States Militia

The Revolution spanned the years 1776 to 1784 and could not have succeeded without the armed citizens of American communities. Approximately five years later, after much debate, the Constitution with the first ten amendments, known as the Bill of Rights, was proposed to the states by Congress. The ratification was completed December 15th, 1791 and declared on March 1st, 1792.[10]

The Second Amendment says: "A well regulated Militia, being necessary to the security of a free State, the right of the people to keep and bear Arms, shall not be infringed." A detailed analysis of the history, origin, and evolution of the Second Amendment can be found in two excellent books, *To Keep and Bear Arms: The Origins of An Anglo-American Right*, by Joyce Lee Malcolm, and *That Every Man Be Armed: The Evolution of the Constitutional Right*, by Stephen P. Halbrook.

After almost two centuries of wars and preparation for wars, against Indians, Spanish, French, and their own overbearing British rulers, Americans understandably feared being disarmed. Therefore, they made their system of defense and the bearing of arms suitable for defense a formally protected, fundamental right of American citizens.

The Militia Act of 1792 passed and became law on May 8th of that year.[11] This law required white males from ages 18 to 45 to become members of their state militias. Every militiaman had to "provide himself with a good musket or firelock."[12] The country correctly feared future invasion and more war when it encouraged citizens to keep arms.

War of 1812

The flintlock continued to play an important role in defense against Indians, and again in battles during the War of 1812. Well over half of the American forces in the War of 1812 were militiamen, who would respond to an alert directed to the part of the country under attack by British troops. Most of the American forces at the battle of New Orleans were militia. The final battle on January 8, 1815 proved the power of American militia against the British Army with their victory over the professional British Army forces. Andrew Jackson, the regular army general commanding the American force, had been promoted from the Tennessee militia.

The forces under Jackson included U.S. Army regulars and Louisiana, Kentucky, and Tennessee militiamen. The militia fielded about 2,000 men equipped with rifles. The riflemen stood four ranks deep behind breastworks, from where they took turns firing. The British Army attacked on January 8, 1815 with "7000 of the best equipped and disciplined soldiers in the world"[13] "After a clash that lasted less than one hour, the British army suffered one of the most humiliating defeats in its military history, losing more than 2000 men of its fighting force." The Americans lost 13 dead and 39 wounded.[14]

Texas

The war for Texas independence in 1836 saw volunteers from many states, especially in the south, go to Texas and become part of the Texas militia. Some of these men defended the Alamo and others, under General Sam Houston, eventually defeated the regular army of Mexico and freed Texas to govern itself.

Mexican War

The United States resolved to admit Texas to the Union in March of 1845, despite knowing that Mexico still considered it part of Mexican territory. On April 25, 1846, troops from the 2,000-man Mexican Army, which had crossed the Rio Grande River into a disputed area of southern Texas (now an American state), and attacked a unit of 70 U.S. Army dragoons (a type of cavalry), killing eleven and capturing the rest, many of whom had suffered wounds.[15]

United States regulars, supplemented by Louisiana and Texas militia, then fought two larger battles with the Mexican Army north of the Rio Grande. These battles, called Palo Alto and Resaca de la Palma, resulted in significant U.S. victories.[16] The United States subsequently declared war against Mexico on May 13, 1845. General Winfield Scott led an Army of regular U.S. soldiers and State militia into Mexico.[17] "In all, 26,922 regulars and 73,260 volunteers (militia) served at some point during the Mexican War."[18] This army fought several battles, culminating in the surrender of Mexico City on September 14, 1847. Hostilities ceased on February 2, 1848.

The Mexican War formally ended when both sides ratified the Treaty of Guadalupe Hidalgo by May 30, 1848. Under its terms, the United States withdrew its forces and paid the Mexican government $15 million. The U.S. also assumed responsibility for about $3.5 million in claims by Americans against Mexico. The Mexicans recognized Texas as an American state. with the Rio Grande as its southern boundary. They also granted much of present day Arizona, California, Nevada, New Mexico, Utah, parts of Colorado, part of Wyoming. and some other territory to the U.S.

American Civil War and Aftermath

The U.S. Civil War, also called the "War Between the States," could not have been won by the North without participation of the militias from the Union states. These men frequently brought their personal firearms or weapons provided by their state for militia use. These often included the earlier flintlock "militia muskets" converted from flint to percussion. The northern states' militias and draftees conscripted into state service provided the majority of the manpower necessary for the North to subdue the Southern "Insurrection." It was during the Civil War that the Union instituted the first national draft in America.

A number of laws attempted to prevent freed slaves from possessing firearms following the Civil War. Southerners feared violence from armed former slaves and possibly wished to continue using force to subdue them without fear that the freed slaves would defend themselves with weapons. Congress enacted the Freedmen's Bureau Act on July 16, 1866 in part to prevent states from disarming former slaves.

Spanish American War

The Spanish American War began after the USS Maine, an American battleship, exploded and sank in Cuba's Havana Harbor. Believing that hostile Spaniards had sabotaged the ship, and committed to supporting Cuban independence, the U.S. demanded that Spain surrender control of Cuba. Madrid declared war against the United States on April 23, 1898, and Washington reciprocated on April 25, 1898.

At the time, the U.S. Army's entire strength consisted of 28,000 regulars. The individual states mobilized 220,000 organized militiamen in units from all over America in response to Spain's declaration of war, and the U.S. War Department accepted many of those state militia units into Federal service. These men fought with regular Army soldiers in Cuba, Puerto Rico, and the Philippines.[19]

World War I

The United States joined England and France to fight in World War I on April 6, 1917. America entered World War I, at least in part, over a threat of invasion by Mexico. On January 16, 1917, The Foreign Secretary of the German Empire, Arthur Zimmerman, sent a coded telegram to the German Ambassador in Mexico proposing an alliance that included German support to help Mexico reconquer its lost territory in California, Texas, New Mexico, and Arizona. The German ambassador delivered the message, now known as the Zimmerman telegram, to the Mexican government.

German efforts to incite invasion of the United States by Mexico, combined with the killing of American civilians on British passenger ships by German submarines, resulted in a declaration of war against Germany. The National Defense Act of 1916, passed in anticipation of possible participation in the war, authorized the President to call National Guard units to Federal service in emergencies.[20] The Selective Service Act of 1917, enacted on May 18, allowed drafting U.S. citizens to serve in units, by state, combined to form the "National Army."[21] By the end of 1918, the military had inducted three million draftees under this Act. The National Guard supplied 40% of the U.S. Combat Divisions during the war.[22] The National Army divisions provided at least that percentage, so most of the American forces were "Citizen Soldiers" or militia.

World War II

During World War II the Combat Division, composed of approximately 15,000 men, served as the primary combat formation of the American Army. The soldiers who made up our over 90 divisions came from four sources. The regular Army had twenty divisions, the state National Guards provided nineteen divisions, the organized Army Reserves contributed twenty-five divisions and the draftees of the "Army of the

U.S." filled the remaining twenty-eight divisions. The National Defense Act of 1916 had created the organized reserves, created Reserve Officer Training Corps (R.O.T.C.) in colleges, and authorized a strong peacetime National Guard of 450,000 men.[23] It also codified the concept of a larger standing Army of regulars (175,000) supplemented when needed by the National Guard and Reserves.[24]

The World War II regular army divisions combined career soldiers (officers and enlisted) with volunteers. National Guardsmen had volunteered for state duty, which included some training, prior to being called to national service. In September of 1940, President Roosevelt ordered the National Guard to Federal active duty to train and mobilize for possible war. When the war began in December of 1941, some National Guard divisions deployed to war zones almost immediately.

Organized Reserve units had volunteer members, many of whom had prior active-duty service, along with ROTC officers and volunteers. These divisions mobilized, trained, and deployed with relative speed. The Army of the U.S., the new name for the National Army of World War I, had Regular Army officers and Non-Commissioned Officers (NCOs) in charge of draftees.

The Selective Training and Service Act of 1940 had authorized conscription of young men for military service in the Army of the U.S. during peacetime.[25] America drafted ten million men under this act and its successor, the Selective Service Act of 1941.[26]

The National Guard mobilization and formation of the Army of the U.S. with draftees, supplemented by huge numbers of volunteers from civilian life, resulted in approximately half of the 16,000,000 U.S. military personnel of WW II acting as militia, or temporary "Citizen Soldiers." Most went back to civilian life after the war and did not serve further in the reserves.

Korea

The U.S. military structure of the Korean War resembled that of World War II. The Army still had units from four distinct organizations, the U.S. Army (regulars), U.S. Army Reserves (USAR), Army National Guard (ARNG), and the draftees in the Army of the United States (AUS). Under the Military Selective Service Act of 1948[27] and the Universal Military Training and Service Act,[28] over 1.5 million male citizens were inducted into the military between June 1950 and July 1953. Another 1.3 million volunteered for service. The National Guard and draftees again represented the militia component of U.S. forces.

Vietnam

Forces of the United States during the Vietnam era again included Regular Army, Reserves, and National Guard, as well as a large number of draftees. The federal government did not order full mobilization of the National Guard, and only 23,000 went on active duty, with 8,700 deployed to Vietnam. The military inducted well over 2 million young male citizens with the draft during the war years.

The government stopped issuing draft orders in early 1973, and the requirement to register ceased in April of 1975. Registration with the Selective Service System resumed in 1980 for male citizens and resident aliens 18 to 25 years old. Severe penalties, including fines up to $250,000 and up to one year of prison, apply to those who do not register. Lawmakers occasionally discuss reinstating a draft, but no plans to do so appear likely, even though the system to do so remains in place.

Modern Militia

The Second Amendment, the Militia Clauses of the Constitution, and the Tenth Amendment, when read together, leave no doubt that the states kept the right and power to call forth, train, and use militia for defense if needed in an emergency. The relevant part of Article I, Section 10 of the Constitution says: "no State shall, without the Consent of Congress, ...keep Troops, ...in time of Peace ...or engage in War, unless actually invaded, or in such imminent Danger as will not admit of delay."

Congress has consented for states to keep two types of troops in time of peace. The National Guard falls under dual control and may be used by a governor, unless that state's troops receive a call to Federal duty. State Defense Forces, authorized by Title 32 of the U.S. Code, may be maintained by states in time of peace. By statute, the U.S. government cannot draft these state forces into Federal service.

National Guard

State militia organizations became the National Guard with the Militia

Act of 1903 (also known as the "Dick Act"). This gave state militias status as the primary Federal reserve force.[29] The Act divided the militia of all able-bodied male citizens between 18 and 45 years old into two categories, the "organized militia," called the National Guard, and the "reserve militia," which later statutes call the "unorganized militia."

The National Defense Act of 1916 gave authority to the Federal government for temporary use of state National Guard during war or national emergency.[30] In addition to providing increased Federal control and funding of the National Guard, the law required each member of the Guard to take a dual oath, one to his Governor and one to the President. This Act allowed the President to draft members of the Guard into Federal service, and mandated that each member "from the date of their draft, stand discharged from the militia, and shall from said date be subject to" the regulations of the Army.[31] This Act also established the Militia Bureau of the United States War Department, required the name "National Guard" for all existing state militia organizations, and included them as part of the Army.[32] The War Department became the Defense Department when the National Security Act of 1947 consolidated the Departments of War, Navy, and Army.[33]

Federalization of the National Guard continued with the National Guard Status Act of 1933, which made the National Guard a permanent component of the U.S. Army, and formalized a "dual enlistment" in both state and Federal service for guardsmen.[34] Use of the National Guard by Federal authorities required mobilization of all the National Guard at this point in time. The United States mobilized all of the National Guard in World War I and again in World War II.

The Selective Service Act of 1948 allowed Congress or the President to call National Guard units to Federal duty as needed for "national security for up to 21 months."[35] Four Army National Guard divisions deployed to Korea on active duty in September, 1950.[36]

The Armed Forces Reserve Act of 1952 provided that National Guard units could stay on Federal active duty as long as required in time of war, national emergency or as "the national security may require."[37]

It also authorized active duty without any emergency requirement, with consent of the governor involved.[38]

The National Guard had become a recognized part of the Army under the Army Reorganization Act of 1950, and the Reserve Forces Act of 1955 included all of the National Guard in the U.S. military category of "ready reserve."[39] These forces would be called next after regular forces to serve in times of conflict. This Act authorized the President to activate up to 1 million ready reservists without a declaration of war or national emergency by Congress. In 1957, the Army imposed minimum training standards for all reserves, including the National Guard.

In April, 1968, in response to the Tet Offensive in Vietnam, President Johnson called 24,500 National Guard and Reserve members to active duty.[40] By December of 1969, over 9,000 National Guardsmen served in Vietnam.[41]

The Total Force Policy Act of 1973 made the National Guard subject to the United States military during peacetime.[42] The Goldwater-Nichols Department of Defense Reorganization Act of 1986 applied further Federal control to the National Guard.[43] The United States Code then authorized the Secretary of Defense to use the National Guard for up to 180 days without state approval or declaration of need by Congress.[44] If Congress declares a national emergency, the entire National Guard or any of its members may be held on active duty for the duration of the emergency plus six months.[45] Under this authority, approximately 75,000 National Guard members served on active duty in the first Gulf War during the early 1990s. The Federal government no longer needed state approval to activate individual Guard members.

Federalization of the National Guard continued with the Defense Authorization Act of 1987, giving Federal control over up to 200,000 National Guard members for involuntary duty for up to 180 days inside the U.S.[46] Congress recently added natural disasters, epidemics or public health emergencies, and terrorist attacks or "incidents" to the events allowing Federal control of the National Guard for service in the Continental United States.[47]

The National Defense Authorization Act of 1996 approved further Federal control of the National Guard.[48] The statute allows the U.S. Congress to approve ordering the National Guard units or individuals to Federal duty and have them retained on Federal duty for as long as needed.[49]

The National Guard has become a Federal military force for deployment worldwide, including duty inside the U.S. for domestic emergencies outside of the units' home states. Hundreds of thousands of Guard members have served in combat zones or disaster areas since 1991. The National Guard has recently responded to calls for disaster duty in Haiti, Bosnia, Kosovo, and America's Gulf States. "The Guard deployed more than 50,000 troops in support of the Gulf States following Hurricane Katrina in 2005."[50] Tens of thousands of Guard members currently serve on active duty.[51]

While nominally still state units, the National Guard frequently cannot serve in their traditional role as state militia for local defense and disaster response because Federal requirements "preempt" state needs. This change of role has occurred gradually over the past 100 years, with formal acknowledgment in 2008.[52]

Perpich v. Department of Defense

U.S. House of Representatives member G. V. Montgomery (D., Miss.) attached an amendment to the bill for the 1987 Defense Budget that changed the requirement for governors to consent for the Army to send National Guard units abroad on Federal duty for non-emergency missions.

Governor Perpich of Minnesota filed suit in Federal court to challenge the constitutionality of the Montgomery Amendment. The Supreme Court upheld the Amendment on a number of grounds.[53]

One of the reasons the Supreme Court gave for finding the Montgomery Amendment constitutional was that ordering the National Guard to Federal service did not take away the state's ability to have a militia. "Congress has provided by statute that, in addition to its National Guard, a State may provide and maintain at its own expense a defense force that is exempt from being drafted into the Armed Forces of the United States.[54] As long as that provision remains in effect, there is no basis for an argument that the Federal statutory scheme deprives Minnesota of any constitutional entitlement to a separate militia of its own."[55]

State Defense Forces

The Federal government authorized creation of state Defense Forces during peacetime to provide a substitute military organization when the National Guard had Federal duty or to supplement the National Guard on state duty, if needed.[56] The National Guard Bureau regulates state defense forces, without necessarily controlling them.[57] While the legal structure for state Defense Forces exists nationally and has been implemented in some states, the number of actual members and amount of training for Defense Forces remain limited.

The modern concept of separate state Defense Forces began in 1933 when the Federal government first required the National Guard to have dual status as both Federal (Title 10) and state (Title 32) troops. Many states had active Defense Forces during World War II, while their National Guard members served on Federal duty overseas. Federal law continues to recognize state militia as separate from the U.S. Armed Forces which, as we have seen, now include the National Guard.[58]

Twenty-one of the fifty states have some version of a state Defense Force organization in place.[59] Most do not require qualification or training for proficiency with weapons. They focus their training efforts on managing unarmed responses to major disasters or other emergencies. The State Guard Association of the United States (SGAUS) operates a National Academy, with the help of the Federal Emergency Management Agency (FEMA), to teach and certify members of state Defense Forces as Military Emergency Management Specialists.[60] Members may also participate in training as part of Community Emergency Response Teams, provided by or through FEMA.[61] These programs do not include any training in armed security, defense, or firearms.

The Draft

Defense Forces let governors of states that have them draft able-bodied citizens into an existing militia organization in an emergency. States without Defense Forces will have to rely upon Federal forces or organize their own force after an emergency occurs. The national militia structure for drafting civilians into Federal military service also remains, with the Selective Service Act and registration of young men authorized by law. Eleven million men currently qualify for the draft under the U.S.

Selective Service system. Another 11 million young women might also be drafted under current law. The U.S. Militia generally includes males aged 17 to 45 years.[62] Virginia includes males aged 16 to 55 years.[63] Both extend ages for military veterans.

The constitutional authority for the Federal draft resides in Article 1, Section 8, which says, in part, "The Congress shall have Power To... provide for the common defense... To raise and support Armies... To provide for calling forth the Militia to execute the Laws of the Union, suppress Insurrections and repel Invasions; To provide for organizing, arming, and disciplining, the Militia, and for governing such Part of them as may be employed in the Service of the United States, reserving to the states, respectively, the Appointment of the Officers, and the Authority of training the Militia according to the discipline prescribed by Congress... And To make all Laws which shall be necessary and proper for carrying into Execution the forgoing Powers." The Federal courts have upheld the draft as a partial calling forth of the militia as recently as 1968. [64]

Conclusion

Many gun control advocates seek to have Americans give up the tradition of armed citizens. Some argue that the militia no longer has a purpose in the 21st century.[65] Others claim that the militia has already vanished.[66] While opinions vary on the purpose of the Federal and state militia, both obviously exist.

The U.S. Constitution, U.S. Code, many state constitutions, state codes, and related regulations still consider "the People" as militia. Under these laws and our historic traditions, as long as it has able-bodied citizens, does America have a militia? If called upon in an emergency to act for community defense, what arms should citizens bring to the "fight," and how will they learn to use them? The next, final chapter addresses these questions.

Chapter 8

SECOND AMENDMENT QUESTIONS

The Modern Citizen Soldier

This chapter gives answers to questions of why we might need militia in the future, advice about what to buy for a Second Amendment rifle, and recommendations related to "keeping and bearing" a firearm suitable for community defense (with secondary self-defense and sporting uses). Comparatively speaking, the recommended rifles act as the modern versions of the militia muskets and hunting rifles of the past.

Has the Militia Become Obsolete or Vanished?

The ancient, fundamental right of citizens to keep and bear arms came to America as a guarantee "which we had inherited from our English ancestors."[1] The Founders included it in the Constitution to preserve the right, in the face of a then-forming central government, to have arms for individual self-defense and the common defense as part of the militia.[2] The Constitution requires consent from Congress for states to maintain troops in peacetime, but states can have troops and engage in war if invaded "or in such imminent danger as will not admit of delay."[3]

"So what if our founders thought they needed arms?" I have been asked, "Why does that matter? Isn't the whole concept obsolete? How could a state in a country with jets, tanks, a modern navy, drones, missiles, and nuclear weapons possibly need armed citizens to serve as militia?" We looked at some answers in Chapter 2, without specific scenarios. Now, let's try a hypothetical set of circumstances.

First, imagine a war in the Far East that draws much of the U.S. Navy, Air Force, and a substantial force of U.S. Army ground troops to the conflict. A new invasion of South Korea by North Korea, for example, or a Chinese attack on Taiwan or the Philippines.

Then consider a simultaneous war in Eastern Europe, the Middle East or Southwest Asia, like an invasion of the Baltic states by Russia or of Lebanon by Syria. Even worse, the Taliban could revolt in Pakistan with the goal of controlling that country's nuclear arsenal. Any of these or similar conflicts could result in deployment of most of America's remaining forces, including the National Guard.

Finally, with most of our forces bogged down overseas, suppose that we have a major event in the Continental United States that overwhelms our remaining forces and police departments, such as a colossal natural or man-made disaster that results in a breakdown of order. Or perhaps a series of coordinated terrorist attacks, designed to take advantage of of our military forces' absence. Something that threatens our freedom, our lives, or even our existence.

Then what? When people ask, "Hasn't the militia system and even the concept vanished?" I answer emphatically, "No, it has not." Millions of private citizens with prior military training could and would serve as "militia." Additional millions have combat and survival skills and abilities, learned through life experiences and private training. If governments did not organize people of this sort for defense in an emergency, they would organize themselves and defend their communities.

Using the Commonwealth of Virginia as an example, the governor, under the "Military Laws of Virginia,"[4] would "call forth" all or part of the state militia to serve during the emergency for "Militia State Active Duty" in the Virginia Defense Force.[5] If the governor decided that the Defense Force members needed weapons to defend themselves or communities, he could and would authorize them to bring firearms.[6]

National Guardsmen not called to Federal duty, current Defense Force members, and newly accepted members with prior military service would assume the positions as officers for this militia, with the governor serving as Commander-in-Chief. While obviously not as effective as our professional military, these thousands or even millions of armed citizens, "well regulated" by experienced officers, could allow the state to restore order and defend its population.

The Virginia Constitution, in Article 1, Section 13 says, in part: "That a well regulated militia, composed of the body of the people, trained to arms, is the proper, natural, and safe defense of a free state, therefore the right of the people to keep and bear arms shall not be infringed…" Virginia does not have a large arsenal of individual weapons on hand to arm its militia, so if the governor authorized arms, citizens would have to provide privately-owned firearms as part of their service. Since the Commonwealth cannot generally afford to pay for training for a huge number of its citizens in the use of firearms, the responsibility for both the purchase of guns and acquiring of the proficiency in their use would fall to the individuals themselves.

The term "militia" has acquired negative connotations in the modern media, both because of its use to describe rebels in other countries and because of non-government groups in the United States who style themselves as militia. In the Constitutional context, the militia includes the National Guard, State Defense Forces, and all citizens capable of acting in defense of community, state, and country. If "the people" had to act as militia, they would do so under the control of officers appointed by the state.

What Gun to Buy?

For many years, and especially lately, people have asked my opinion on the best gun to buy. Many of these folks have never before owned a firearm, but for a variety of reasons have decided to purchase one. I have always responded to their questions with one of my own: "Why do you want one?" Their answers dictate my advice.

Target shooting often calls for a .22 rimfire rifle or pistol; clay pigeons require a shotgun in one of the skeet gauges; and the optimum hunting gun depends upon the game. Making the "best" choice for self-defense depends upon whether the defensive scenario would occur inside the home, outside the home, or both. Many firearms can have multiple purposes, although each use normally has at least one preferred design.

Rifles

A responsible citizen who wants to prepare for defending his or her community should purchase and become proficient with a bolt action rifle. American forces have used this design on the battlefield in every conflict from the Spanish-American War in 1898 to Iraq and Afghanistan. Simplicity, reliability, and accuracy make a bolt action ideal for learning and use by citizens who are unfamiliar with modern service rifles such as the AR-15, the M-1A, and the M-1 Garand.

Experienced, trained citizens will usually have semi-automatic service rifles, and supplementing them with large numbers of bolt actions in capable hands would present a formidable force. Additionally, mass shootings and bans have created both social stigma and, in some states, legal barriers to owning semi-auto "assault weapons." A modern service rifle could easily replace your bolt action rifle (except where illegal), once you become comfortable with shooting and owning a rifle.

Experts differ in opinions as to the best firearms to have for weapons, depending upon the individual's circumstances and the expert's own experience. Sidearms (pistols and revolvers) have important roles in defense, as do shotguns, large caliber rifles, and other firearms. After long study and much consideration in the 1980s, the U.S. military decided that the M-16 rifle would best serve as the primary individual weapon for everyone in a combat role. Because of its ease of use, relatively low cost, legal availability, accuracy, and power, a bolt action rifle also makes an excellent choice for militia purposes.

Our armed forces and law enforcement use bolt action rifles to place accurate fire on hostile targets from fairly close range to over 1,000 yards. Civilians can purchase similar rifles all over the United States. Browning, Mossberg, Ruger, Remington, Winchester, and Savage immediately come to mind as dependable American manufacturers.

The rifle should have a matte or parkerized finish on metal parts, with a dull-finish synthetic or wood stock. Ideally, it should use .308 Winchester (7.62 NATO) ammunition, with .223 Remington (5.56 NATO) as a close second choice. While the .308 provides better long range and penetration capabilities, it has significant recoil when fired. People of slight stature should choose the .223, which has very little recoil. Comfortably firing a .308 requires a tough shoulder or thick padding. If in doubt, start with the .223.

I prefer these two calibers because they use ammunition commonly available in civilian markets, as well as being the standard calibers used by the U.S. military. Standardization of calibers has great benefits in combat, because troops can share weapons and ammunition. However, many other calibers will work for community defense. If the only rifles available come in other calibers, one cardinal rule of defense is that any rifle is better than no rifle. Just make sure to have enough ammunition on hand, and that the caliber's specifications make sense for defense purposes (not too little power or too much recoil).

Accessories

Ideally, the rifle should have open or "iron" sights, with the possible addition of a mounted telescopic sight or "scope." Iron sights work better at close ranges and in low light, as well as surviving wet weather and other abuse better than the more fragile riflescopes. However, many if not most bolt action rifles made today do not have open sights, and come with scope mounts only. If you can find a model with open sights -- and a few do exist -- buy it instead of a scope-only model.

Scopes and mounts should have matte or "flat" finishes that do not reflect light. The mounts usually come with the rifle, but if you have to buy them separately, make sure they fit the rifle, have the correct scope tube diameter and are the right height to allow mounting. Available scopes range from inexpensive, fixed-power models to several-thousand-dollar variables with on-board computers. I recommend a lower cost, American-made variable power scope in 3-to-9 power with a 40mm diameter objective (front lens). The one depicted in the photo below would work well. Called the Leupold Vari-X I, 3-9x40 Tactical, this model was designed for law enforcement use. It is the sight on the Ruger Model 77, .223 Remington caliber law enforcement and tactical bolt action rifle shown in the illustration below.

Ruger, Model 77

Your rifle needs sling swivels and a good leather or web sling (carry strap). This allows you to carry the rifle slung over your shoulder and also provides stable shooting support for better accuracy. A carrying case also comes in handy, to protect the rifle during transport. It should have side pockets for ammunition and cleaning gear.

Cleaning equipment must include a sectional cleaning rod, bore brushes, patches, patch jag (for pushing patches through the rifle's bore), bore solvent, gun oil, and cleaning rags. Every rifle requires cleaning as soon as possible after firing (Always be sure to unload your firearm before cleaning!). Failure to clean your rifle will result in corrosion inside the bore, which degrades the rifling and reduces accuracy.

Other accessories could include a bipod, like the one in the photo, a few basic small tools and, if appropriate, extra magazines. Most bolt action rifles have integral or "fixed" magazines holding five or six rounds, but a few, like the new Mossberg MVP FLEX, take detachable magazines. If your rifle has separate magazines, you should buy several extras with up to the maximum capacity legally available in your state, but no more than 30 rounds each. Military personnel typically carry a minimum of seven 30 round magazines for the M-16, one in the rifle and three in each of two belt pouches. This gives a soldier 210 rounds before needing to reload magazines. While armed citizens could make do with less, this seems a good approximate guide to how much ammunition to carry.

I suggest purchasing only American-made ammunition. Patriotism aside, foreign ammunition can have corrosive properties and may have suffered damage from improper storage. For each rifle, you will need ammunition for practice and at least two to three hundred rounds for possible emergency use. I recommend a 500-round case as the initial purchase, and 1,000 rounds would not hurt. The reasonable quantity for a mix of practice and potential tactical capacity falls between 200 to 300 rounds on the low side to as high as 2,000 to 3,000. Combat troops expecting battle each add hundreds of extra rounds to their basic load, carrying them in backpacks.

Bullets for practice include match, hunting, or military ball, but do not expect match ammunition to perform well in tactical situations. Match bullets usually have thin, fragile jackets and weak internal construction. They often will not penetrate even the slightest barrier. Military ball (full metal jacket or FMJ) or solid base hunting bullets work better for defense.

Ammunition will last almost indefinitely, if stored properly. Much like fine wine, it fares better at steady temperatures in the 45 to 55 degrees Fahrenheit range. Steadiness of temperature matters because swings between hot and cold produce condensation and chemical reactions in gun powder. Extreme heat will make the powder deteriorate more rapidly. I like to use military metal ammo cans, available at many surplus stores and gun shows. I store the cans inside a locked metal storage locker, kept where temperatures are steady and (for the sake of safety and security) *away* from my rifle storage area.

Storage

I cannot overemphasize the importance of safe, secure storage for your rifle. While FBI statistics show that criminals seldom use rifles in homicides, compared to other types of weapons, no responsible citizen will allow a thief, a child, or the mentally ill to have access to firearms.[7] I recommend four practices, and/or a combination thereof, to prevent misuse. These include gun safes, alarm systems, concealment, and disabling. Modern gun safes will prevent access by children, most mentally ill people, and some criminals. However, determined criminals with burglar tools can eventually break into any safe, if given enough time.

Keys and combinations also require security to prevent unauthorized opening. Don't hide them in obvious places. I like to hide my safe combinations or keys in pockets of clothing in a very full closet away from the room containing the safe. Only I know which pocket the combinations are in, and it would take anyone else days to go through all of the clothes in the house.

Higher quality safes stand up to fire or cutting efforts longer than inexpensive versions, but all work to some extent. Sporting goods stores and online businesses have safes of all sizes and prices. Ideally, you would use a double-walled, fire and burglar-resistant model. Most gun safes have bolt holes for securing them to a wall and/or floor, which makes them more difficult to break into. Even a low cost sheet metal box with a key lock offers better security than a closet corner, glass door gun cabinet, or wall rack.

Since all safes have some vulnerabilities, I prefer to combine their use with an alarm system. The best systems have a monitoring station to call police when the security breach signal goes out. They have battery back-up and cellphone or radio back-up, so cutting telephone wires or power lines cannot defeat them. A simple wireless motion detector in the room containing the gun safe provides some coverage. Of course, systems for entire residences have fire, water, glass break, and opening sensors available. The simplest version sets off an alarm when a door is opened, and costs very little.

Some people may find that the expense of safes and alarm systems makes their use unrealistic. Cost-free approaches include concealment. In other words, keep the rifle well hidden. A thief cannot take what he cannot find. Also, do not talk about having a rifle (or any guns) with anyone who does not have a real need to know about it.

You can easily remove the bolt from a rifle and secure or hide it in another location. Before the Federal government took full control of the National Guard, it used this method to control its weapons. Until the 1980s, Federal officials kept all bolts or some other critical part of every weapon at a separate, off-site, secure facility. Some units had their rifle bolts stored in local police department safes. Others went to U.S. Army Reserve vaults. I remember when my Guard unit needed training or qualification with weapons, a Federal officer would bring the bolts to the Armory, then retrieve them after training and cleaning. Citizens can use a similar system to assure no one ever uses their rifle for criminal purposes. *Do not* trust children, even your own, and especially teenage boys, with access to usable firearms and ammunition, unless you are absolutely sure of their ability to handle them responsibly.

Clothing and Equipment

Anyone defending his or her community as contemplated by the Second Amendment becomes a temporary soldier. That means dressing like a soldier and having the necessary gear to function as one. This starts with the rifle, its accessories, and ammunition, but you need to acquire other basic items, as well.

Necessities include load-bearing equipment (LBE) to carry the accessories, ammunition, and everything else. Web gear, vests, packs, and pouches can come from military surplus or sporting goods stores that carry hunting and/or hiking inventories. Don't buy anything colorful, shiny, or bright, however. The LBE also allows you to carry the food, water, clothing, shelter, and personal items needed for several days of "duty."

Do not forget personal medications, a first aid kit, and toiletries for field sanitation. Include a sturdy knife and a working flashlight. You should pack as if expecting a long backpacking trip to hunt large game for days with primitive camping. Pre-pack everything in a single duffle, large backpack or other "go bag" that you can grab, along with your rifle, on relatively short notice.

Canteens and a minimal mess kit will help with food and water. Include water purification chemicals and consider what food makes sense. I suggest military meals, ready to eat (MREs) or freeze-dried hiking foods. Consider adding a portable entrenching tool, a military grade gas mask, and, if you can afford one, a night vision device.

If your state has a Defense Force, find out what uniform its members wear, and buy one. If not, military surplus uniforms or camouflage hunting clothes will work.

Skill Development

Having all of the equipment for emergency defense will not help unless you have the skills to care for yourself and use the gear properly. As Henry Cabot Lodge recognized in *The War with Spain*, learning the right skills and practicing them so as to become nearly a soldier in ability has served American citizens well in past conflicts.[8] This allows patriotic civilians to form into capable fighting units quickly and effectively.[9]

The best training combines educational or academic study with practical "hands-on" activities. Start by taking classes. The NRA Basic Rifle Course fits perfectly for beginning shooters. So do classes taught by the Boy Scouts, 4H, shooting schools, and Civilian Marksmanship Program rifle clubs.

After World War II, and continuing until today, the Defense Marksmanship Program (DMP) has provided many thousands of M-1 carbines, 1917 Enfields, M1 Garands, 1903 and 1903A3 Springfield rifles to civilians for rifle practice and possible use for defense. The National Defense Act of 1916 authorized the War Department to distribute arms and ammunition to civilian rifle clubs. It also provided funds for operation of rifle ranges and opened military rifle ranges to civilian shooters. Many military ranges still serve civilian shooting clubs.

The Army administered the related Civilian Marksmanship Program (CMP) for rifle and pistol competition from 1916 to 1996, when a non-profit corporation charged specifically with this purpose took over all CMP programs.[10] These programs are designed to help citizens develop proficiency with firearms, in case they have to serve in the traditional role of citizen soldiers. You can find a CMP club by going to their website[11] and clicking on "Find a CMP Affiliated Club" in the text. Fill in the blanks for your area city and state. Choose "Open" under membership. For the best training results, start with one of the "3 Position" programs and then move to a "Highpower" program. (The 7.62 and 5.56 NATO are considered highpower calibers.)

The hundreds of available books and thousands of magazine articles that describe rifle shooting and individual tactics can help you learn. Books and manuals about sniper training also describe skills you may need; consider reading as many as possible. Videos, audio books and Internet sites can help develop knowledge.

The study of shooting should go beyond basic marksmanship. Learn to "sight in" a rifle. This means adjusting the sights so that the visual aim point and bullet impact point match at a certain range. I suggest 100 yards for beginning high power shooters. Also learn cleaning techniques, and make sure to clean your rifle after every shooting session. Then move to basic soldier skills like navigation with map and compass (GPS may not function during an emergency), outdoorsmanship, communication (without cell phones) and first aid. Be sure to understand camouflage, cover, and concealment. Also study tactical movements found in basic infantry training manuals, like "rushes," "low crawls" and "high crawls." Know how to prepare an individual fighting position that provides you with maximum visibility of potential targets, concealment, and cover, then practice enough to become proficient (at least once).

Practice and practical activities develop and refine skills – academic study alone cannot suffice. You have to physically perform these actions at least a few times to fully develop them. Start with target shooting. I highly recommend a second rifle for this purpose.

Consider buying a bolt action .22 rimfire with sights similar to your primary rifle. While it cannot replace the larger caliber, with which you must still practice, it uses inexpensive, lower noise, no-recoil ammunition. I train beginning rifle shooters with a .22 bolt action single-shot using open sights. As the student's shooting skills develop, the .22 continues to provide low cost, less complicated practice. Air rifles can also serve to learn basic skills.

Joining a rifle club and participating in shooting competitions would help with more advanced marksmanship skills. So would a "precision rifle" course at one of the shooting schools. America has many of these academies to help military and law enforcement personnel and private citizens improve their skills. Examples include Professional Firearms Training (PFT) in West Virginia and Montana, the U.S. Shooting Academy in Oklahoma, Front Sight in Nevada, Thunder Ranch in Oregon, Gunsite in Arizona, Thompson Long Range in Utah, Defensive Edge in Idaho, Premier Rifle Academy in California, the Firearms Academy of Seattle, Washington, Universal Shooting Academy in Florida, and many others. The website www.martialfirearmstraining.com lists 316 schools in 43 states. Once you master the basics, I recommend a trip to one of these schools for advanced training.

Hands-on activity should include far more than shooting. If, in an emergency, you act to help defend your community, you will need at least some of the other soldiering skills. Try backpacking and primitive camping. Consider participating in orienteering (a land navigation competition). Learn to use radios for communication. Consider becoming a hunter, especially pursuing game hunted with an accurate rifle at longer ranges. Any activity with elements of outdoorsmanship and physical endurance will help.

Don't expect to learn all you need to know immediately. It takes one to two years of nonstop training and practice to become a proficient soldier. An armed citizen who tries hard to learn and has no military experience will need several years to become effective as a temporary citizen soldier. Proper diet and regular exercise have as much importance here as they do in any athletic endeavor. If you can't move and have no stamina, you can't function as a soldier, even temporarily. If you have the financial resources but not the physical ability to train yourself, consider funding the training and equipment for a physically capable family member.

You could join the National Guard or Army Reserves to receive formal military training. If you make this choice, ask for infantry training, but be ready for Federal service overseas.

Planning

If you want to act as a responsible armed citizen, you must plan. First, plan to take care of yourself in an emergency, so that law enforcement does not have to protect you. Besides, in the event of a significant crisis, local authorities could face overwhelming problems and not have the capacity to respond to individual emergencies. Also, plan to protect your family, both for their safety and to avoid overburdening law enforcement. Finally, make plans for the security of your family without you, if possible, in the event that you are called upon to help defend the community. If this final contingency is not possible, you will of course stay with your family and secure your home or whatever location you have chosen.

The first issue for any emergency preparedness plan involves deciding whether to stay ("shelter in place") or go to a safer location ("evacuation"). The wisest plan allows for both, depending upon circumstances. If you stay, plan a "safe room" with necessary supplies, communications, and security measures, in which you and your family can be as secure as possible.

Evacuation requires even more planning. Ideally, you will know where to go, and will have made arrangements to live there temporarily. A second residence, family member, or trusted friend could provide a safe haven. Regardless of destination, you need a primary planned route and multiple alternative routes, should your primary escape route be rendered impassable or excessively dangerous to travel.

Most people who evacuate will attempt to use vehicles and drive the public roads. This risks road blocks, vehicle failures, attacks, and accidents that could leave you on foot. Prepare to walk, even if for days. That means packing a travel "go bag" for each person with the essentials to proceed on foot. By all means, pack as many containers of food, water, and supplies as possible in the vehicles, but you might have to abandon anything that your party cannot carry.

You should study vehicle defense tactics to learn where and how to carry your rifle while traveling. Many of the shooting schools teach mobile defense techniques.

The Federal government, most state governments, and a number of other organizations provide good emergency preparedness advice and planning resources. The Federal Emergency Management Agency (FEMA) maintains two websites that suggest plans for preparedness;[12] so does the Federal Center for Disease Control and Prevention;[13] and the American Red Cross.[14] Many states have similar web sites with information specific to the state.

Unfortunately, none of these organizations include physical security and self-defense plans, even though we face the possibility of armed looters, criminals, or terrorists attacking families in their homes or during evacuation. But if you combine their advice with that of this chapter, you can include an active self or family defense strategy in your emergency preparedness plans.

Consider training, practicing, and planning with another person. The "buddy" concept has long worked well in the military. Your spouse, another family member, or a neighbor could help improve and shorten preparation time for both of you. During my Army experience, buddies helped each other constantly. We took turns guarding and sleeping, shared food and supplies, and divided labor. Buddies often save each other's lives in battle. Now, in addition to the other aspects of married life with children, my wife (also prior military) and I support each other to provide family security.

Once you and your family have achieved personal security in a safe location, community defense comes next. Assuming that your family's safety does not require you to stay with them, plan for acting as a citizen soldier in a unit with the purpose of community defense. The "well regulated militia" of the past called for family, friends, and neighbors to combine for training and combat. These forces need to be "roughly, quickly, and effectively moulded into a fighting regiment by the skillful discipline" of their officers.[15]

Individuals or groups should attach themselves to existing forces or select officers to follow and create their own local units. State Defense Forces, if available, provide the appropriate structure. County sheriffs have traditionally acted as organizers of local defense. State Police, National Guard and Federal forces could also provide armed citizens with the discipline, support, and structure needed for area defense.

Regardless of the ultimate force composition, armed citizens who act as soldiers have to work together as units. Large-scale defense requires skillful teamwork and a clear chain of command. Military units of any type, including militia, cannot succeed without discipline. If you cannot follow the orders of officers appointed to lead you, stay home. Prepare a communications plan before you need it, and remember that workable communications must remain available long after e-mail, cell service, telephone lines, and media access have failed.

The most important community defense goal for an armed citizen in a severe emergency revolves around becoming an asset rather than a liability to those charged with local security. If you have neither the equipment, the self-discipline, nor the skills to help with defense, you may become a hindrance or a burden. If acting as a responsible, armed citizen appeals to you, please expend the time, money, and effort necessary to do so competently.

Conclusion

Gun Control

It's a well-documented fact that some citizens have proven themselves to be incompetent, suicidal, criminal, or insane. Some have even shown themselves to be violent, even homicidal. Common sense makes it obvious that people like this should not have firearms. The fear of becoming a victim of one these "prohibited" persons is what really motivates the anti-gun effort, and it is a fear that is easy to understand. Unfortunately, many advocates of gun control would restrict or disarm everyone, in hopes of affecting the prohibited persons.

Gun control theory holds that limiting certain types of arms or their magazine capacity will reduce the death toll in a mass shooting. In truth, marginal reductions in lethality cannot accomplish much, if anything. It is far too easy to circumvent bans, and simple, old fashioned guns remain deadly. That's why England eventually banned all firearms after a mass shooter used a double-barreled shotgun and a .22 rimfire bolt action rifle, both 19th century designs, to murder his victims. Gun control cannot accomplish its goal of using laws to prevent violence with guns unless all firearms come under government supervision, affording government full control of both the possession and use of firearms.

Anti-gun advocates want citizens to stop having arms to defend themselves and their communities, considering the idea as obsolete and too dangerous with modern weapons. At least some believe in a policy of total civilian disarmament, like that implemented in England and Australia, and in using the one-step-at-a-time, progressive method to gradually eliminate the possession of all firearms by private citizens.

I recently listened to a panel discussion on National Public Radio about gun control that had been held shortly after James Brady died. The on-air commentators lamented that President Obama had failed to "move the ball" on guns, despite the opportunity to "advance the agenda" after Sandy Hook. The discussion moved to the Brady Act, which requires background checks for dealer transactions. They considered the law important because it provides "something to build upon" in the fight against guns.

With this being the anti-gun advocates' prevalent attitude, supported by the existence of a number of sophisticated organizations with major funding, gun control proponents stand ready for another attempt to "move the ball." Universal background checks (tracing), assault weapons bans, and magazine capacity limits will remain likely targets, as the groups and their spokespersons take aim at the Second Amendment.

The Second Amendment

Private citizens' willingness and ability to come together for the common defense was always at the core of the Second Amendment, along with individual self-defense. This protective strategy, born of centuries of experience, provides a failsafe in case of sudden, unexpected violence in a dangerous and uncertain world.

However, since the early 20th century, the right to bear arms for self-defense and for collective defense by service in the militia, protected by the Second Amendment, has changed in one major aspect. Originally intended as the primary source of protection and defense, armed citizens have become a back-up or emergency alternative to law enforcement and the professional military.

The ability to defend themselves and their families gives millions of Americans a sense of security that they are determined to keep, as the founders intended. Many fear letting government have a monopoly on the use of armed force for a number of reasons, and adamantly oppose complete civilian disarmament. Removing all firearms from civilians in the U.S. cannot happen legally without repeal of the Second Amendment. For such a repeal to be implemented, three-fourths of the states would have to ratify it. Obviously, the opponents of such a measure are in a strong position.

Showdown

There exists no national consensus on the advisability of more gun control, largely because there are strongly held opposing views on the role of civilians in protecting themselves from violence. People who would like only law enforcement and the military to have guns occupy one extreme, while those who believe that all capable citizens should possess whatever firearms they desire, and know how to use them, represent the other end of the spectrum. Both extremes have passionate, vocal minorities who advocate their positions.

The majority of citizens fall somewhere in the middle. This group includes many Americans who do not own firearms, and who rely entirely upon government forces for their protection. To these people, all-encompassing national policies that apply to everyone might seem reasonable, or at least acceptable approaches to prevent crime or mass shootings. On the other hand, these citizens do not automatically support all gun control and many of them see the value of responsible citizens having arms for self and community defense.

The majority also includes millions of gun owners who see restrictions on their ability to defend themselves and their families as unacceptable. Gun control proposals that fall short of damaging them directly, like universal background checks, do not particularly worry these citizens, until they realize that the new laws actually represent progressive steps toward the realization of a broader anti-gun agenda. When that agenda is fully understood, the ultimate goal of total government control over firearms does affect both their sense of independence and their need for the ability to provide for their own safety.

Advocates on the extremes try hard to sway large segments of the middle to their points of view. One side uses emotional appeals to sympathy for the victims of the violent criminal acts committed with firearms, playing upon people's fears that they could be next, to advance its agenda. The other side focuses on people's fear of losing the ability to defend themselves and their loved ones against acts of violence.

Anti-gun groups whittle away at gun ownership, striving to eventually disarm all civilians, while the pro-gun organizations support expanding gun rights wherever they can, with each side's efforts serving to feed the opposing side's fears. I believe that we should focus on practical solutions to the misuse of guns, and stop indulging in endless, expensive, and ultimately futile political debate over gun control. Posturing and fear-mongering do not serve to make us safer or more free. They only keep us more divided.

A more reasonable approach

Education about firearms safety, training for better security, and more effective law enforcement responses would help to make us safer. Secure storage of firearms to prevent their theft, safe gun handling practices, and active security measures would also help immeasurably. So would improving our system of mental health diagnosis and treatment. All of these ideas cost money, time. and effort, which are currently being wasted in the highly-politicized but fruitless arguments over gun control and the Second Amendment.

Unfortunately, forces on both sides appear to invest all their energy and resources into the next serious clash or "showdown" between gun control and the Second Amendment, ignoring measures that could actually enhance our safety.

I hope that you have found this book informative and useful, and that it has helped you understand the facts, the law, and the arguments in the gun debate. If you have found the book useful, I hope that you will tell your friends and family about it. I would also appreciate reading your reviews of the book on www.amazon.com. And if you would like to receive email updates about what is happening in the ongoing debate and legal wrangling, please subscribe to my e-newsletter on gun control and the Second Amendment at www.guncontrolbook.com. I promise you that your email address will never be sold, rented, or shared with anyone.

All my best,
Lenden A. Eakin

Endnotes

Chapter 1

1. 48 Stat. 1236, 1934
2. 307 U.S. 174, (1939)
3. *Commentaries on the Laws of England*, by Sir William Blackstone, Volume 4, Chapter 11, paragraph 9 (1769)
4. Dangerous and Unusual Misdirection, by Daniel R. Page, May 4, 2011, www.works.bepress.com/daniel_page/1
5. 52 Stat. 1231, 1938
6. *The Torch is Passed*, Associated Press Production, by Edward T. Fleming, p. 13
7. Id., p. 15
8. Id., p. 22
9. Id., p. 62
10. "Oswald: The Disappointed Revolutionary," by Peter Savodnik, *The Wall Street Journal*, October 5, 2013, p. C1, C2
11. Id.
12. "Firearms and Federal Law: The Gun Control Act of 1968," by Franklin E. Zimring, *Journal of Legal Studies*, 4 (1975): 133
13. Pub. L. 104-208, 18 U.S.C. 1922(g)(9)
14. ATF Form 4473 (5300.09) Part 1, OMB No. 1140-0020
15. The Right to Keep and Bear Arms Report, Subcommittee on the Constitution, Committee on the Judiciary, United States Senate, 97th Congress, 2nd Session, February 1982, p. 23
16. California Stats. 1989, Chapter 19
17. Pub. L. 103-322, 108 Stat. 1796
18. Id.
19. www.alerrt.org
20. www.change.gov/agenda/urbanpolicy-agenda
21. www.whitehouse.gov/issues/urban-and-economic-mobility
22. "Obama to Seek New Assault Weapons Ban," by Jason Ryan, ABC News, February 25, 2009

Chapter 2

1. *The Wall Street Journal*, December 18, 2012, p. A17
2. "Rise of the Warrior Cop," by Radley Balko, *The Wall Street Journal*, July 20, 2013, p. C1
3. Id.
4. "The Truth About 'Second Amendment Remedies': How To Counter Insurrectionists Arguments, Educational Fund to Stop Gun Violence," www.efsgvxessgv.org
5. "Smith & Wesson's Owners Target Value," *The Wall Street Journal*, June 25, 2013, p. C1
6. "J. P. Morgan to Call Business Clients," *The Wall Street Journal*, October 9, 2013, p. C1, C2
7. www.csgv.org
8. Id.
9. *Gun Fight: The Battle for the Right to Bear Arms in America*, (1999) by Adam Winkler, pp. 447 and 448
10. Id.
11. Id.
12. Id., p. 35

13. “Bloomberg Plans Gun-Law Ads,” *The Wall Street Journal*, March 25, 2013, p. A4
14. “Obama Tries to Jump-Start Gun Push,” *The Wall Street Journal*, April 3, 2013, p. A6
15. www.whitehouse.gov/issues/preventing-gun-violence
16. Department of the Treasury, Bureau of A.T.F. & E, TD ATF 391, 95R-05(P)
17. https://www.youtube.com/watch?v=Pvf7wVsAp60
18. Aaron Hawkins, www.wnd.com
19. “Guns, Mental Illness and Newtown,” by David Kopel, *The Wall Street Journal*, December 18, 2012, p. A17
20. Id.
21. Id.
22. “The Final Report and Findings of the Safe School Initiative,” Washington, D.C., May 2002, www.secretservice.gov/ntac-ssi
23. Id., p. 27
24. Id., p. 28
25. Kopel, *The Wall Street Journal*, December 18, 2012
26. “Physicians’ Groups Say Nuclear Threats Are Even Greater Today Than in the Past,” by Tracy Hampton, PhD, *Journal of the American Medical Association* (JAMA), Vol. 308, No. 7, Aug. 15, 2012, p. 660
27. Id.
28. www.armscontrol.org
29. Id.
30. Defense Science Board, “Assessment of Nuclear Monitoring and Verification Technologies,” January 2014, www.acq.osd.mil/dsb/reports2010.htm
31. JAMA
32. *The Wall Street Journal*, January 22, 2013, p. A18
33. “How North Korea Could Cripple the U.S.,” by R. James Woolsey and Peter Vincent Pry, *The Wall Street Journal*, May 21, 2013, p. A17
34. “About That New ‘Moderate’ Iranian Cabinet,” by Soharb Ahmari, *The Wall Street Journal*, August 8, 2013, p. A11
35. “Without Stronger Sanctions, Iran Will Go Nuclear,” by Mark Kirk and Eliot Engel, *The Wall Street Journal*, 8/13/13, p. A15
36. “Israel is Letting Its Guard Down,” *The Wall Street Journal*, July 19, 2013, p. A11
37. “Regrouped Al Qaeda Poses Global Threat,” by Adam Entous, *The Wall Street Journal*, August 5, 2013, p. 1
38. “How Al Qaeda Made Its Comeback,” by Ali Soufan, *The Wall Street Journal*, August 8, 2013, p. A13
39. *The Wall Street Journal*, Entous
40. *The Wall Street Journal*, Soufan
41. Id.
42. “Assault on Power Grid Raises Alarms,” by Rebecca Smith, *The Wall Street Journal*, February 5, 2014, p. 1
43. Id.
44. Id.
45. JAMA, p. 661
46. Chapter 1, “Of the Absolute Rights of Individuals,” Book 1, Rights of Persons, by William Blackstone, 1769

47. Id.
48. Id.
49. Id.
50. "A Citizen of America: An Examination into the Leading Principles of the Federal Constitution," by Noah Webster, The Debate on the Constitution, Part One, Literary Classics of the United States, New York, N.Y., 1993, p. 154
51. Id., p. 155
52. "'The Republican' to the People: The Principal Circumstances Which Render Liberty Secure," The Debate on the Constitution, p. 710, 712
53. Thomas Jefferson
54. *The Debate on the Constitution*, Part 1, p. 578
55. "The U-Boat Rocket Program," www.prinzeugen.cou/v2
56. "Japanese Super Sub," www.pbs.org/wnet/secrets/features/japanese-supersub
57. "False Alarms in the Nuclear Age," by Dr. Geoffrey Forden, November 6, 2001, www.pbs.org/wgbh/nova/military/nuclear-false-alarms
58. Id.
59. Id.
60. "Conservatives Become Targets in 2008," by Kimberly A. Strassel, *The Wall Street Journal*, May 24, 2013, p. A11
61. "The IRS and the Drive to Stop Free Speech," by David B. Rivkin, Jr. and Lee A. Casey, *The Wall Street Journal*, May 21, 2013, p. A17
62. "A Radical Departure on Press Freedom," by Theodore J. Boutrous, Jr., *The Wall Street Journal*, May 24, 2013, p. A13
63. "What We Lose if We Give Up Privacy," by Peggy Noonan, *The Wall Street Journal*, August 17, 2013, p. A13
64. Id.
65. "Obama Suspends the Law," *The Wall Street Journal*, August 17, 2013, p. A13

Chapter 3

1. "Six Months After Newtown, Connecticut ~ A New Political Landscape on Guns," by Rema Levy, International Business Times, June 14, 2013, www.ibtimes.com
2. p. 9
3. p. 16
4. p. 30
5. p. 49
6. p. 56
7. p. 68
8. p. 40
9. p. 43
10. Id.
11. Id.
12. Levy, op.cit.
13. "Firearms Curbed in Colorado," by Ashby Jones, *The Wall Street Journal*, March 21, 2013, p. A3
14. "New Push to Confiscate Firearms," by Jack Nicas, *The Wall Street Journal*, 7/27/13, front page

15. Id., p. A5
16. "Guns, Mental Illness and Newtown," by David Kopel, *The Wall Street Journal*, December 18, 2012, p.A17
17. "Categories of Persons Prohibited from Receiving Firearms," TD ATF-391, C.F.R. 95R-051P, effective August 26, 1997
18. 45 CFR, Part 164
19. *The Wall Street Journal*, Nicas, p. A5
20. Id.
21. "Pro-Gun Laws Gaining Ground Since Newtown," by Jack Nicas and Joe Palazzolo, *The Wall Street Journal*, April 4, 2013, p.1; p. A4
22. Id., p. 1
23. "Delicate Workplace Issue: Guns in the Parking Lot," by Sara Murray, *The Wall Street Journal*, October 16, 2013, p. B1, quoting the Law Center to Prevent Gun Violence
24. Id., p. 88
25. Va. Senate Bill 1335
26. *The Wall Street Journal*, Nicas and Palazzolo, p.A4
27. *The Wall Street Journal*, Kopel, December 18, 2012
28. "Some Schools Rely on Armed Staff," *Gun Digest*, September 9, 2013, p. 13
29. Id.
30. "Injury and Violence Prevention" by Hahn, et al, *American Journal of Medicine*, 2005:28 (2SI) p. 40
31. Id., p. 43
32. Id., p. 48
33. Id., p. 50
34. "Support Grows for Vote on Gun control Bill," by Kristina Peterson, *The Wall Street Journal*, April 10, 2013, p. A5
35. "Path Opens for Gun-Control Bill to Reach Senate Floor," by Patrick O'Connor and Sarah Portlock, *The Wall Street Journal*, April 1, 2013, p. A4
36. "Obama Tries to Jump-Start Gun Push," by Colleen McCain Nelson, *The Wall Street Journal*, April 3, 2013, p. A6
37. "GOP Senators Pushed to Join Gun Filibuster," by Janet Hook and Kristina Peterson, *The Wall Street Journal*, April 5, 2013, p. A5
38. "The Promise," by Matt Bennett, The Third Way, Brookings Institute
39. "Support Grows for Vote on Gun-Control Bill," by Kristina Peterson, *The Wall Street Journal*, April 10, 2013, p. A5
40. "The Gun Rights Consensus," *The Wall Street Journal*, editorial, April 19, 2013, p. A14
41. "Obama Takes Senate to Task for Failed Gun Control Measure," ABC News, April 17, 2013, abcnews.go.com
42. Fox News, April 17, 2013, www.foxnews.com
43. *The Washington Post*, April 18, 2013
44. April 17, 2013, Rose Garden speech
45. *The Wall Street Journal*, April 19, 2013
46. Id.
47. *The Wall Street Journal*, June 25, 2013
48. "Newtown Gun Permits Surge," by Joseph DeAliva and Alison Fox, *The Wall Street Journal*, August 1, 2013, p. A3

49. Id.
50. "Kansas CCW Permits Double," *Gun Digest*, August 12, 2013, p. 13
51. "Permits Soar to Allow Guns to Be Concealed," *The Wall Street Journal*, July 5, 2013, p. A3
52. Id.
53. Id.
54. "Second Amendment Skirmishes," *The Washington Times*, March 25, 2013, www.washingtontimes.com/news/2013/mar/25
55. "The Promise"
56. July 14, 2013
57. Guide, p. 40
58. Id., p. 44
59. Id., p. 41
60. www.nytimes.com/2013/03/29/us/rewards-by-president-obama-on-gun-violence
61. Id.
62. Navy Yard Shooting Remarks, Marine Barracks, September 22, 2013
63. Id.
64. Id.
65. Id.
66. "American Sovereignty and Its Enemies," by Sohrab Ahmari, *The Wall Street Journal*, July 20, 2013, p. A13
67. Id., quoting former Senator Jon Kyl, R-Arizona
68. Id.
69. Id.
70. under "Use of Terms," (f) "Tracing"
71. "Obama's United Nations Backdoor to Gun Control," by John Bolton and John Yoo, *The Wall Street Journal*, April 15, 2013, p. A17
72. Art. VI, U.S. Constitution
73. Senate Amendment 139 to Senate Constitutional Resolution 8, March 3, 2013
74. "National Regulation of Small Arms," IANSA, 2006, www.iansa.org
75. "Prevention of Human Rights Violations Committed with Small Arms and Light Weapons," Human Rights Council, U.N. General Assembly, July 27, 2006, p. 4, www.refworld.org/docid/45c30b560.html
76. Id., p. 14
77. Id.
78. Id.
79. EU Directives, 91/477/EEC, 2008/51/EC
80. Id.
81. Ahmari, *The Wall Street Journal*, July 20, 2013, p. A13
82. "Joe Biden Readies Gun Control advocates for Round Two," April 25, 2013 www.huffingtonpost.com/2013/04/25/joe-biden-guns
83. "Connecticut Governor Calls for Expansion of Gun Laws," by Joseph DeAvila, *The Wall Street Journal*, February 22, 2013, p. A3
84. "Obama's Gun-Control Misfire," by Kimberly Strassel, *The Wall Street Journal*, April 5, 2013, p. A13
85. Rose Garden speech, April 17, 2013

86. Id.
87. *The New York Daily News*, April 18, 2013
88. Strassel, April 5, 2013
89. "Obama Takes Senate to Task for Failed Gun Control Measure," ABC News, www.abc-new.go.com/Politics, April 17, 2013
90. www.everytown.org
91. www.theenoughcampaign.com
92. Obama Remarks on Gun Violence, January 16, 2013, www.foxnews.com/2013/01/16
93. www.politico.com/magazine/story/2014/05/nra

Chapter 4

1. *Gun Fight: Guns in America* (1999) by Winkler, p. 33
2. Special Gun Show Issue, *Gun Digest*, June 3, 2013, Vol. 30, Issue 12, F&W Media, Inc., Iola, Wis.
3. "Off Target," by Dan Baum, *The Wall Street Journal*, February 16, 2013, p. C1
4. Winkler, p. 22
5. www.gallup.com/poll/161813
6. Id.
7. Inaugural Address, January 21, 2013
8. Id.
9. www.whitehouse.gov/the-pres-office/2013/04/03
10. President Obama's Speech on Gun Control Bill Defeat, April 17, 2013
11. *The Personal MBA*, by Josh Kaufman, Portfolio/Penguin, New York, N.Y., 2010, pp 155-6
12. HTTP://blogs.rollcall.com/wgdb/arms-treaty-stymied-by-2nd-amendment-concerns-in-senate
13. "Summary of Select Firearm Violence Prevention Strategies," by Greg Ridgeway, Ph.D., Deputy Director, National Institute of Justice, January 4, 2013
14. *U.S. v. Abramski*, 706 F. 3d 307, No. 11-4992, 4th CIR., 2013
15. www.supremecourt.gov/oral-argument-transcripts/12-1493__2135pdf. p. 52, lines 8-12
16. Id., p. 53, lines 11-12
17. Ridgeway.
18. p. 178
19. Id., p. 179
20. pp. 624-5
21. *Peruta v. County of San Diego*, February 13, 2014
22. Ridgeway.
23. Id.
24. Id.
25. Baum, *The Wall Street Journal*, p. C2
26. Id.

Chapter 5

1. *Soldiers of the Virginia Colony: A Study of Virginia's Military, Its Origins, Tactics, Equipment and Development*, by D. A. Tisdale (2000) p. 2

2. Id. p. 17
3. Jamestown Museum, Jamestown, Virginia
4. *Flintlock Guns and Rifles: An Illustrated Reference Guide*, by F. Wilkinson, Ames, and Armour Press, London (1971) p. 9
5. Id.
6. Id., p. 11
7. Id., p. 15
8. www.snipercentral.com/snipers
9. Alamo Museum, San Antonio, Texas
10. *The Evolution of Military Rifles*, U.S. Army Infantry School, March, 1969, p. 2
11. Id., pp. 2-3
12. Id., p. 3
13. Id., p. 3
14. www.apstudynotes.org/us-history/topics/end-of-the-frontier
15. *Battles That Changed Warfare: 1457 B.C.–A.D. 1991*, by Kelly Devries, et al., Metro Books, New York (2011), p. 137
16. www.pattonhq.com/garand
17. *U.S. Military Firearms*, by Major James E. Hicks, James E. Hicks, & Son, La Canada, CAL, p. 118
18. *The M16*, by Jean Huon, Casemate, Havertown, PA, 2004, p. 28

Chapter 6

1. *Operator's Manual for Rifle, 5.56mm*, TM9-1005-249-10, Department of the Army, Washington, D.C., 1990
2. www.ar-15.com and www.ar-15.us
3. www.odcmr.com/nm/history
4. P.L.104-106, Feb. 10, 1996, Sec.1601-1624
5. CMP NLU#776, 17th Edition, 2013
6. www.whitehouse.gov/the-press-office/2013/08/29/fact-sheet-new-executive-actions
7. 36 USC § 40728A. Recovery of Excess Firearms
8. 4/8/2013 speech
9. *District of Columbia v. Heller*, 554 U.S. 570, 582 (2008)
10. Id., p. 662
11. Id., pp. 634-5
12. *To Keep and Bear Arms: The Origins of an Anglo-American Right*, by Joyce Lee Malcolm, Harvard University Press (March 6, 1996), p. 156-7
13. *Heller*, pp. 624-5
14. Id., p. 636
15. *U.S. v Miller*, 307 U.S. at 139
16. *D.C. v Heller*, 554 US.S 70, 627 (2008)
17. *People v. James*, 94 Cal. Rptr. 3d 576 (2009)
18. Cal. Stats. 1989, Ch. 19
19. *People v. James*, p. 585
20. Id., p. 586
21. "The Lockstep Justices," *The Wall Street Journal*, February 28, 2013

22. "Massive Gun Resistance," *The Wall Street Journal*, April 13, 2013, p. A14
23. "Democrats Rein in Senate Filibusters," by Janet Hook and Kristina Peterson, *The Wall Street Journal*, November 22, 2013, p. 1
24. "Obama Lobbied for Filibuster Change," by Peter Nicholas and Janet Hook, *The Wall Street Journal*, November 23, 2013, p. A5
25. Hook & Peterson, p. 1
26. "Least Dangerous Branch," by Randy Barnett, *The Wall Street Journal*, November 20, 2013, p. A11
27. Id.
28. Id.

Chapter 7

1. www.oxforddictionaries.com/us/definition/american__english/militia
2. p. 595, quoting *Miller*
3. *Soldiers of the Virginia Colony: 1607-1699*, by D.A.Tisdale, 2000, p. 54
4. www.britishbattles.com/braddock
5. www.britishbattles.com/battle-of-ticonderoga
6. *Flintlock Guns and Rifles*, by F. Wilkinson, Arms and Armor Press, London, 1971, p. 15
7. *Bunker Hill*, by N. Philbrick, Viking Press, New York, N.Y., 2013, p. 222
8. Id., p. 281
9. http://www.britishbattles.com/battle-yorktown.htm
10. *Debate On The Constitution*, The Library of America, 1993, p. 984
11. www.constitution:org/mil/mil-act-1792
12. Id.
13. "A Long Rifle With General Andrew Jackson," by Mark Sage, *American Rifleman*, June, 2013, p. 68
14. Id., p. 69
15. "Mexican American War: Roots of the Conflict, 1836-1846," by Kennedy Hickman, http://militaryhistory.about.com/od/mexicanamericanwar.
16. "The U.S. Army Campaigns of the Mexican War, Along the Rio Grande, Palo Alto and Resaca de la Palina, U.S. Army Center of Military History," www.history.army.mil/html/books/073/73_2/CMH_Pub_73-2.pdf
17. "The U.S. Army Campaigns of the Mexican War, Gateway South, The campaign for Monterrey, U.S. Army Center of Military History," www.history.army.mil/brochure/The_Campaign_for_Monterrey.htm p. 9
18. "The American Army in the Mexican War: An Overview," www.pbs.org/kera/usmexicanwar/war/american_army.html
19. "U.S. Order of Battle," 1898 www.spanamwar.com
20. usacac.mil/cac2/call
21. www.legisworks.org/congress/64/publaw-85.pdf
22. Id.
23. 39 Stat. 166, Ch. 134, June 3, 1916
24. Id.
25. www.legisworks.org/congress/80/publaw-759.pdf
26. www.gpo.gov/fdsys/pkg/STATUTE-65/pdf/STATUTE-65-Pg75.pdf

27. www.legisworks.org/congress/57/session-2/publaw-33.pdf
28. www.legisworks.org/congress/64/publaw-85.pdf
29. Id.
30. Id.
31. www.legisworks.org/congress/80/publaw-253.pdf
32. Id.
33. www.legisworks.org/congress/80/publaw-759.pdf
34. www.arng.army.mil/aboutus/history
35. www.constitution.org/uslaw/sal/066_statutes_at_large.pdf, p. 481, 489
36. Id., p. 490
37. P.L. No. 66-476, 1952
38. Id.
39. P.L. 305, August 9, 1955, uscode.house.gov/statutes
40. Exec. Order No. 11406
41. www.loc.gov/frd/pdf-files/cngr
42. usmilitary.about.com/cs/guardandreserve
43. PL-99-433
44. 32 U.S.C. 904
45. 10 U.S.C. 12301(a)
46. 100 Stat. 3816, P.L. 99-661, November 14, 1986
47. 32 U.S.C. 502 (f)
48. Public Law 104-106, 2/10/1996
49. 32 U.S.C. Sec. 102
50. www.usmilitary.about.com/od/guardandreserve
51. Id.
52. *National Guard Domestic Operations*, NGR 500-1/ANGI 10-8101, June 13, 2008, www.ngb-pdc.ngb.army-mil/pubs/500/ngr500_1
53. 496 U.S. 334, 1990
54. 32 U.S.C. §109 (c)
55. Id., p. 352
56. 32 U.S.C. 109
57. 32 U.S.C. 109) (c)
58. 10 U.S.C. 311
59. www.statedefenseforce.com
60. www.MEMSACADAMY.WEBS.com
61. www.FEMA.GOV/COMMUNITY-EMERGENCY-RESPONSE-TEAMS
62. 10 U.S.C. §311- Militia: Composition and Classes
63. Va. Code §44-1
64. *U.S. v. Holmes*, 387 F2d 781, 7th Cir., Cert. Denied.
65. www.guns.com/2012/05/12debate-ladd-everitt-coalition-to-stop-gun-violence/
66. *The Second Amendment: A Biography*, by Michael Waldman, Simon and Schuster, N.Y., 2014, p. 81

Chapter 8

1. *Robertson v. Baldwin*, 165 U.S. 275, 281 (1897)
2. *Heller*, p. 599
3. Article I, Section 10
4. Va. Code, Chapter 44
5. Va. Code Sec. 44.75.1
6. Va. Code Sec. 44-54.12
7. www.fbi.gov/about-us/cjis/ucr/crime-in-the-u.s./2011/crime-in-the-u.s.-2011/tables/expanded-homicide-data-table-8
8. *The War with Spain*, by Henry Cabot Lodge, Harper Brothers, New York and London, 1900, p. 114
9. Id.
10. www.odcmp.com
11. www.odcmp.com/clubs/searchclubs.htm
12. www.ready.gov and www.fema.gov/preparedness
13. www.emergency.cdc.gov/preparedness/plan
14. www.redcross.org/prepare
15. *The War with Spain*, Lodge, p. 114

About the Author

Lenden A. Eakin writes as an attorney with over thirty years of firearms-law experience. He also has a sideline business as a federally licensed firearms dealer (FFL) and teaches gun safety, self-defense and marksmanship as a certified instructor for rifle, pistol, shotgun, and personal protection.

Lenden first qualified as "expert" with the M-16 rifle during R.O.T.C. training at the College of William and Mary in the 1970s. While an officer in the U.S. Army and Virginia Army National Guard, he often supervised rifle and pistol ranges as the Officer-in-Charge. He also repeatedly qualified again as "expert" with the M-16 service rifle, as well as service pistol. Eakin currently consults with other attorneys as a firearms expert in litigation matters and interprets gun control proposals for a number of legislators from both parties.

He lives with his wife, Kimberly, a recently retired Army Reserve firearms instructor and former active duty member of the Army Marksmanship Unit, and two children. Family hobbies include baseball, swimming, hunting, and of course, target shooting.

Lenden's late father, G. Ralph Eakin (1919-2010) served thirty-three years with the Virginia State Police. He was a firearms instructor, competitive shooter on the department's national pistol team and a sniper on its first SWAT team. Over a dozen close relatives have served in law enforcement and/or military, in all branches of service.

Lenden A. Eakin's training, education and experience make him uniquely qualified to understand and explain the "Showdown" between gun control and the Second Amendment.

INDEX

S

Cases

Federal Statutes

Federal Regulation

State Statutes